Architecture of Middle Tennessee

Architecture of Middle

Tennessee

The Historic American Buildings Survey

Vanderbilt University Press

Nashville, 1974

Edited by

Thomas B. Brumbaugh

Martha I. Strayhorn
and
Gary G. Gore

Photographs by

Jack E. Boucher

Ro 24171

Produced with the Co-operation of
the Historic American Buildings Survey
of the National Park Service

Library of Congress Cataloguing-in-Publication Data

Brumbaugh, Thomas B   1921–
    Architecture of Middle Tennessee.

    Based on an exhibit of photos. and drawings from
the Historic American Buildings Survey presented at
Vanderbilt University.
    Includes bibliographies.
    1. Architecture—Tennessee, Middle. 2. Tennessee,
Middle—Historic houses, etc.   I. Strayhorn, Martha I.,
1925–   joint author. II. Gore, Gary G., 1931–
joint author. III. Historic American Buildings
Survey. IV. Title.
NA730.T4B78   917.68′03′5   72–2879
ISBN 0–8265–1184–8

The Historic American Buildings Survey

The Historic American Buildings Survey (HABS) is a national program created to assemble a comprehensive record of the building arts in the United States. Formally organized as a co-operative effort of the National Park Service, the Library of Congress, and the American Institute of Architects, the Survey—which has just commemorated its fortieth anniversary—is the federal government's oldest operative historic preservation program.

Although early HABS recording in Tennessee did not delve deeply into the state's rich architectural patrimony, the geographical distribution was well balanced. Log and stone structures characteristic of the eastern third of the state, as well as imposing antebellum mansions of West and Middle Tennessee, such as the Hermitage, were recorded in the 1930s. Perhaps the most impressive early recording effort resulted in a set of twenty-three sheets of architectural measured drawings of William Strickland's State Capitol in Nashville.

World War II forced a temporary halt to the Survey's active recording program throughout the country. By the late 1950s, however, several significant additions—primarily photographs and written historical and descriptive data—were made to the HABS Tennessee collection at the Library of Congress. During this period important measured drawings were also made of the President Andrew Johnson House in Greeneville and of several structures in the Great Smoky Mountains National Park, as part of the National Park Service's "Mission 66" program which was initiated in 1957. Many records were obtained on structures in the historic town of Greeneville which, collectively, give an idea of the character of the community. These records in a way may be regarded as a prototype of the urban neighborhood and area surveys that HABS frequently conducts today.

While some additional recording of historic Tennessee buildings took place in the 1960s, it was not until the 1970s that one of the Survey's most intensive statewide recording efforts was organized. Discussions leading to this ambitious project were initiated in 1969 by William T. Alderson, then a member of the HABS Advisory Board and Director of the American Association for State and Local History. As the program evolved, the Tennessee Historical Commission, local historical groups, and the Survey entered into co-operative agreements to record historic Tennessee structures. Five summer projects, from 1970 to 1974, were scheduled. The first, in 1970, was centered in Nashville and its immediate vicinity. Sponsored by the Commission, the Historic Sites Federation of Tennessee, and HABS, the project included several mid- and late-nineteenth-century commercial structures—a building type heretofore unrecorded in the state.

In 1971, the Middle Tennessee project was undertaken. This survey concentrated on many of the large antebellum mansions of the central section of the state. In 1972, the West Tennessee Historical Society joined the Commission and the Survey in sponsoring the West Tennessee project. Headquartered at Memphis State University, the team produced documentary records for several late-nineteenth-century churches and domestic structures in Memphis, Savannah, Bolivar, and LaGrange.

vi   The 1973 recording team surveyed the eastern third of the state. The Commission, the East Tennessee Historical Society, and HABS co-operatively sponsored the project. Earlier recordings in East Tennessee had concentrated on pioneer structures; the 1973 team recorded later nineteenth- and early twentieth-century structures. The final East Tennessee project in 1974 preceded the publication of a HABS Tennessee Catalog which lists the complete holdings in the state for the first time since 1959.

The awareness in Tennessee of the state's rich historic resources—as evidenced in the continuing support of the Historic American Buildings Survey—has produced some of the finest documentary records in our collections at the Library of Congress. Tennessee is to be commended.

JOHN POPPELIERS
Chief, Historic American Buildings Survey

Preface

THIS book is a celebration of the architecture of Middle Tennessee from its beginnings to 1920. It is a co-operative project of Vanderbilt University Press and the Historic American Buildings Survey of the U.S. Department of the Interior's National Park Service. The book is based primarily upon photographs, measured drawings, and historical and architectural information assembled by HABS researchers on historic buildings in Middle Tennessee during the summers of 1970 and 1971. The Middle Tennessee survey, part of a project meant to encompass the entire state, was sponsored and supported by the Tennessee Historical Commission, Robert A. McGaw, President, and the Historic Sites Federation of Tennessee, Albert Hutchison Jr., Chairman, in co-operation with the Historic American Buildings Survey. William T. Alderson, Director of the American Association for State and Local History, working closely with both organizations, was instrumental in the promotion and support of the project from its inception.

The book is a miscellany with no pretense to being a fully representative or complete record; these buildings, however, are certain to commend themselves to those who love Tennessee, architecture, and superb architectural photography.

Less than two centuries after the first penetration of the Tennessee wilderness, many important early landmarks of the region have been carelessly and wantonly destroyed. Others will soon disappear, but in photographs something of the aesthetic and historic distinction of these surviving monuments can be understood. It is to be hoped that their "preservation through documentation," the stated program of the Historic American Buildings Survey, might also be assisted here.

Twenty years ago it would have been unthinkable that Ryman Auditorium, the Werthan Bag Company of Nashville, or the tobacco warehouses of Clarksville might one day vie for attention with Andrew Jackson's Hermitage or the splendid mansion Rattle and Snap. Nonetheless, the re-evaluation of American culture which is going on today, and the resulting catholicity of current taste, has underscored the significance of such structures for our time. Forts, barns, factories, churches, theaters, and stores were dedicated to the proposition that American enterprise must necessarily be housed in monumental and functional architecture; and thus was expressed a basic sense of form, growing out of the American experience. Of the thirty-five buildings illustrated in these pages, only fifteen are private houses, and four are houses of worship. The others represent a significant number of commercial, industrial, and academic structures.

For modern taste, no doubt the most directly appealing of all the buildings illustrated here are those private houses erected before classical, Gothic, or Italianate motifs appear to distract us. Cragfont near Gallatin, Rock Castle in Sumner County, and Wynnewood at Castalian Springs are extraordinary in their simplicity, and not one of them is the conventionally "beautiful" picture-book home. With them, "Less is more," as Mies van der Rohe would have it, and Tennessee's early builders understood that "modern" principle because it grew out of an intuitive response to human needs and the nature of available materials serving those needs.

Preface

Horatio Greenough, the first American sculptor, writing home from Europe before 1843, thought that if we could

carry into our civil architecture the responsibilities that weigh upon our ship-building, we should ere long have edifices as superior to the Parthenon, for the purposes that we require, as the Constitution *or the* Pennsylvania *is to the galley of the Argonauts. Could our blunders on terra-firma be put to the same dread test that those of ship-builders are, little would be now left to say on this subject.*[1]

In such a context, the Judge John Overton house, Travellers' Rest (1799), must be appreciated. It is shown here freshly clapboarded, its classic understatement reminding us of "Greek principles, not Greek things," in Greenough's phrase. Possibly another Greek principle, hubris, occurred to the learned builder of Travellers' Rest when he settled himself and his family on an Indian graveyard in a tract near Nashville once known as Golgotha.

Less than a generation after most of the buildings shown here were genuinely new, Emerson would observe in *Society and Solitude* that great art depends upon the organic and the useful, a "fitness . . . so inseparable an accompaniment of beauty that it has been taken for it." Thus, from his own words, the "excellent symmetry" of Wynnewood's chimneys, the "purposeful" textures of the ashlar in General Smith's Rock Castle, or the "purgation of superfluities" in Cragfont's façade might be read as the messages of spirit.

Fairvue, west of Gallatin, is the perfect example in brick of a *retardataire* Georgian-Federal building manner which came to Tennessee in the 1820s and 1830s. It is reminiscent of late eighteenth-century Charleston and Virginia grandeur, which is perhaps not quite at home in a more rugged landscape but which represents the social and aesthetic aspirations of wealthy second-generation pioneers. Fairvue was designed in 1832, as a great showplace, and it still serves that purpose today. Its first owner, Isaac Franklin, probably relied on his personal taste and self-taught building skills to act as his own architect. The identical front and rear façades of the main block of the house are embellished with Ionic double porticos and well-proportioned fanlighted doorways, which once looked out over a plantation of some 2,000 acres.

The Hays-Kiser house, near Antioch, and Wessyngton, southeast of Springfield, are comparatively modest houses of late Federal type. Wessyngton's original aspect is still clearly distinguishable behind mansard roofs and the appealing sprawl of later additions, but the Hays-Kiser house stands today sternly reduced to its earlier form. To reveal the original structure gives it new life, so that it is no doubt viewed with fresh vision; yet one may regret the peeling away of a century and a half of hard-won character. The interior of the house is especially distinguished for its marbelized paneling and crisply carved mantels, which are in the local vernacular and suggest that sculpture in

1. Greenough's essay on "American Architecture" was first published in the *United States Magazine and Democratic Review*, XIII, No. 8 (August 1843), 208.

Tennessee was only a dormant art. A further preoccupation with low relief is seen in the exquisite detailing of early furniture made by those same joiner-sculptors who valued texture, proportion, and linear clarity above all else. Their simplifications of Hepplewhite and older colonial patterns perfectly complement the Federal-come-lately rooms.

By 1820, America's taste for Greek things began to express itself in ways ranging from Fourth of July orations to steam engines. In Tennessee, it reached an ultimate architectural fulfillment with William Strickland's State Capitol, designed in 1845, one of the finest Greek-revival buildings at home or abroad. Tennessee's Capitol is "the most elegant, correct, convenient, and genuine public building in the United States, a conspicuous testimonial of the wealth, taste, and liberality of the State," as Andrew Jackson's biographer, James Parton, described it, not too extravagantly, in 1857. In his *History of Davidson County, Tennessee*, Professor W. W. Clayton further quoted Parton as admiring its prospect of the "coiling Cumberland" and "the panoramic valley, dotted with villas and villages, smiling with fields, and fringed with distant, dark, forest-covered hills."[2] It is a landscape taken from a Grecian idyll, and certainly no American hill was ever more beautifully templed.

Monumentally conceived, the Capitol design is balanced by graceful rhythms and proportions in the windows and columns, with the most careful and restrained detailing of Ionic capitals, flutings, and moldings seen in the porticos. Strickland may have been the only architect of the period who was capable of thus using every subtle adjustment to enhance the dignity of a structure which he believed, no doubt correctly, was his major monument. A year before his death in 1854 and ten years after the Capitol commission was given him, Strickland prepared a vault for himself in the east wall of the north portico, where he is buried.

The principal interior stairway and the great halls of the Capitol are uncompromisingly severe, but they lead to the old library—now the Legislative Lounge—where an extravagant amount of wrought-iron work in rococo-revival style is a charming accent. Designed in 1858 by H. M. Akeroyed, the old library represents a major use of this hybrid manner so popular for interior decoration just before the Civil War. Fortunately, the main fabric of Strickland's masterpiece had been completed when a number of naive additions were thus attempted.

By contrast with the severe harmonies of the State Capitol, the tiny Carter House, built at Franklin some fifteen years earlier, is a remarkable back-country example of classicism. It is more famous as a relic of the Civil War battle which raged around it, but its precise Doric details set against Flemish-bonded brick and stepped-gable ends also give it distinction. Seeing it from either side, one might at first glance think that he had come upon a late Jacobean Virginia house on the order of Bacon's Castle in Surrey County. The use of monumental interior proportions marks the house as curiously naive in effect, and even in these days of avant-garde "environments" and complex uses of space in the arts, it

2. W. W. Clayton, *History of Davidson County, Tennessee, with Illustrations and Biographical Sketches of Its Prominent Men* (Philadelphia: J. W. Lewis and Co., 1880), p. 209.

is something of a surprise to walk through the large-scale Carter House sitting room and parlor and ascend its elegant stairway to discover cabin-size sleeping lofts.

We may never be certain whether William Strickland, his rather shadowy assistant and son, Francis, or some other architect designed and executed Belmont in 1850. Its mixture of Italian villa form and Greek Corinthian detail is representative of the new cosmopolitan taste of wealthy merchants and planters who admired small-scale palazzi at Vicenza or Fiesole while on the grand tour. Pattern books by Calvert Vaux, Andrew Jackson Downing, and others confirmed what the travelers had seen and made it intelligible for local builders, and besides, as Downing wrote at mid-century in his book on landscape gardening and rural architecture, the style was eminently practical for expanding American families.

A villa however small . . . may have an elegant and expressive character, without interfering with convenient internal arrangements, while at the same time this style has the very great merit of allowing additions to be made in almost any direction, without injuring the effect of the original structure; indeed such is the variety of sizes and forms which the different parts of an Italian villa may take, in perfect accordance with architectural propriety, that the original edifice frequently gains in beauty by additions of this description.[3]

Certainly the occupants of Belmont must have congratulated themselves on their good taste while reading Downing's account of the style and its effect.

The modern Italian style recalls images of that land of painters and of the fine arts, where the imagination, the fancy, and taste, still revel in a world of beauty and grace. The great number of elegant forms which have grown out of this long cultivated feeling for the beautiful in the fine arts,—in the shape of fine vases, statues, and other ornaments, which harmonize with, and are so well adapted to enrich, this style of architecture,—combine to render it in the fine terraced gardens of Florence and other parts of Italy, one of the richest and most attractive styles in existence. Indeed we can hardly imagine a mode of building, which in the hands of a man of wealth and taste, may, in this country, be made productive of more beauty, convenience, and luxury, than the modern Italian style; so well suited to both our hot summers and cold winters, and which is so easily susceptible of enrichment and decoration, while it is at the same time so well adapted to the material in the most common use at present in most parts of the country,—wood. Vases and other ornaments, may now be produced in our cities, or imported direct from the Mediterranean, finely cut in Maltese stone, at very moderate prices, and which serve to decorate both the grounds and buildings in a handsome manner.[4]

3. Andrew J. Downing, *A Treatise on the Theory and Practice of Landscape Gardening, Adapted to North America* (New York: A. O. Moore and Co., 1859), pp. 336–338.
4. *Ibid.*

Two Rivers, at the junction of the Stone's and Cumberland rivers east of Nashville, is just such a house, although it greets the visitor with a sternly symmetrical double portico, unrelieved today by the large trees, shrubs, and formal gardens which once were planned to ease the approach. Italian baroque was its inspiration, but that luxurious style seems to have been interpreted there by Calvinist carpenters who set up the monumental square columns in a kind of colonnade, crowning them with a heavy entablature. A deep cornice decorated with coffers and doubled brackets ties the composition securely onto the two-story brick mass. The "old home," of painted brick, dating from 1802, still stands nearby, attesting to an extraordinary change of taste during fifty years. Driving through the Shenandoah Valley and across Tennessee, one often sees these parent structures of log or stone, reminders of simpler beginnings, unashamedly preserved as tenant houses or woodsheds beside grand houses of a later period.

At Oaklands, in Murfreesboro, the early-nineteenth-century farmhouse was sufficiently massive to allow the addition directly to it of a rather chaste and effective Italian Lombard façade of about 1855. Saved from vandals in what were very nearly its last days, Oaklands, with the great formal spaces of its three parlors, is also haunted by the surrender there, in 1862, of General T. T. Crittenden, Commander of Union forces in Murfreesboro, to General Nathan Bedford Forrest. Braxton Bragg, Leonidas Polk, and Jefferson Davis were others who lent their historical presence to the structure during grave times, and we are not surprised to learn that the happiest aspect of the house, its ample porch, was built some thirty years later.

Italianate themes are given innumerable variations in such modest houses as that of the architect Adolphus Heiman, or the anonymous Worker's House reproduced here. The top-heavy balance of late-sixteenth-century Florentine palace façades was also to be adapted for the distinguished Morgan-Reeves Building (1856) which stands on Nashville's Public Square, along with some later Italianate storefront survivals. Its Medicean aspect was singularly appropriate for the selling of wholesale dry goods and notions, in a period when the moral fiber of historic styles was so often given serious consideration. Even so, it is instructive to look back a quarter of a century to the Poston Block in Clarksville, where grocery and furniture businesses were suitably conducted behind modified English, or perhaps Philadelphia-inspired, shop fronts. For too long a time it has been assumed that nineteenth-century businessmen such as these were aesthetic boors, when it should have been apparent that their coping with economic realities was inevitably related to their shrewd artistic judgments.

By contrast with familiar English and Italian derivations, the Gothic revival seems an alien style in Middle Tennessee. No doubt it was an imported northern taste for the American South, just as it had been an exotic one in southern Europe. High-pitched roofs are always an affectation where snows are light and quickly melt away. Excellent clay deposits everywhere in the South made brick construction scarcely more expensive than the board-and-batten Gothic houses which characterize the nineteenth-century landscape north of Virginia. Gothic in brick and stone was explored from time to time, especially for places of worship and academic buildings, but without much conviction before 1870. The Episcopal Church in the South encouraged variants of English parish church designs, and Nashville's Church of the Holy Trinity of 1852 is a most successful example. The New York firm of Wills and Dudley designed Holy Trinity with a battlemented tower and buttresses of native limestone, and the interior is enriched with a hammer-beam support system of dark cedar. Adolphus Heiman's old Main Building for the University of Nashville (1853; later the Children's Museum) was another important early use of the genre, and the student who entered its forbidding stone portals must have done so not only with a firm resolve but also very much aware of the gravity of higher education.

After the Civil War, one must reckon with the full-blown Victorian Gothic of such buildings as Fisk University's Jubilee Hall. Described as "modern English" in Clayton's *History*, Jubilee Hall was auspiciously dedicated on January 1, 1876, "in the presence of a vast audience of both races," and the grounds were named Victoria Square "in grateful acknowledgment of kindness shown the singers and friends of the enterprise in Great Britain." Its complex gables, dormers, chimneys, and an asymmetrical pointed tower suggest, as much as anything, a domesticated version of Chambord's French Renaissance roof line. The six-story brick structure is rhythmically decorated with tall windows and belt courses of white stone. Handsomely placed, the building still dominates the modern campus, an expression of exuberant good taste in the era of General Grant.

Just a few years later, Vanderbilt University erected a marvelous gymnasium which is another excursion into a personalized form growing out of the ideas of Sir Charles L. Eastlake, John Ruskin, and Peter J. Williamson of Nashville. "The Old Gym" is also lightly seasoned with elements of the French second-empire style. The interior has been rebuilt to house the Vanderbilt Fine Arts Department, but the little building valiantly resists successful adaptation and yields to no other as a conspicuous landmark.

And in Cockrill Bend, on the south bank of the Cumberland River, six miles from downtown Nashville, the Tennessee State Penitentiary remains an awesome evocation of a medieval fortress with great donjon towers, its well-known silhouette seen from the distant highway looking like one of the Duc de Berry's chateaux in the *Très Riches Heures*.

All nineteenth-century revivals were romantic flirtations with the past, but in Nashville's Union Station we have a serious attempt to reproduce the weight and authority, if not the archaeology, of the Romanesque style. The building is constructed of rusticated Bowling Green gray stone and Tennessee marble and roofed with dark slate. Tall dormers to the height of the roof emphasize its elaborate fenestration, and a tower 239 feet tall rises from the street façade. Directly beneath it, a now unused porte-cochere, decorated with low-relief carving and iron work, once served visitors arriving by train as a formal entrance to the city. For half a century, every traveler passing through on a social or commercial mission must have sensed to some degree the civic pride and authority represented by Union Station. Today, it is in peril from the wreckers, an island in the midst of automobile traffic hurrying to the airports which helped to seal its doom. The main waiting room, with its "art-glass" skylight, is surely one of the richest interiors of the period. Now heavily begrimed and abandoned by all but a ticket agent and a customer or two, the massive building still retains an aura of majesty from an earlier day.

The train-shed to the rear, with its tremendously wide roofs, is an even more monumental structure. The undisguised engineering of its steel beams delights the rational eye and reminds one of the vast supporting timbers and clerestory of the Grange tobacco warehouse at Clarksville, built only a generation earlier. One calls to mind the Apulian cathedrals of Romanesque Italy and, beyond them, the gable-and-clerestory tradition of Roman basilicas erected in the first centuries before Christ. It is a comforting testimony to the nature of man and his works that a method of building should reach our point in time scarcely changed through sixty generations. With such consolation, even the demolition of Clarksville's noble "Elephant Warehouse"—a structure much like the Grange Warehouse—in the spring of 1971 seems less painful, although it is difficult to forget that much of the old pressed brick was, incongruously, shipped to Florida and used in Disney World.

Occasionally, late Victorian buildings are so eclectic or experimental in form that it is reckless to categorize them. The old Federal Building in Clarksville, now used as the Department of Electricity, is dated 1898 on its cornerstone, which suggests that its eccentricities might represent an aspect of the then current and extravagant art nouveau taste. The outstanding architects of the nineties were everywhere demonstrating their impatience with conventional revival styles—sometimes with bizarre results. It should be noted, too, that the Montgomery County Courthouse across the street is an uninhibited second-empire structure which offered considerable competition to any other building designed for the area. The Federal Building's glazed terra-cotta elements were adapted from sixteenth-century Italian mannerist architectural designs as interpreted and adapted in the Netherlands. They serve as little more than a base, however, for the pyramidal copper roof. Large sculptured eagles at each of its four corners hold heraldic shields, and angular projections lead the eye up to an elaborate cupola. One local citizen assured the writer that it was copied from an oriental pagoda, and a more perceptive adolescent gave directions to "the one with the electric roof."

Leafing through this collection, one sees reflected something of the vigor of Tennesseans as builders during more than a century. Here are the monuments of self-reliant men who worked fiercely to subdue the wilderness and at the same time anxiously sought respectability and reassurance in historic models. Here, too, are curiosities of taste—naive, sophisticated, ostentatious, severe things—works expressing contradictions of many kinds, provoked by various social, religious, and economic pressures. Above all, these houses and churches, warehouses and halls are expressions of the freedom and integrity of the individual human self and thus are to be treasured and revered.

Preface

We may still be inclined to give our sentimental attention to such self-conscious creations as Belle Meade Mansion or Strickland's Egyptian-revival Presbyterian Church, even though practical observation tells us that the Public Arcade between Fourth and Fifth avenues, North, or the Second Avenue commercial district is more indicative of the spirit of the century. Nashville still compares herself with dead Athens, that most cruelly vandalized of ancient cities, but one day she might well discover a model in living Amsterdam, devoted for centuries to getting and spending, while jealously preserving a heritage of magnificent halls, houses, churches, synagogues, docks, and warehouses, which are an eternal wealth and glory.

THOMAS B. BRUMBAUGH

Nashville, Tennessee
March 1973

Acknowledgments

The idea for this book originated with Gary G. Gore, Design and Production Manager for Vanderbilt   xv
University Press. Mr. Gore saw, in the Vanderbilt University Fine Arts Gallery, an exhibit of some
of the superb photographs and drawings from the National Park Service's Historic American
Buildings Survey of Middle Tennessee, and he found these materials "so good, so important, and so
appealing," that he began immediately to do everything he could to encourage their publication.

The photographs that appear here are the work of Jack E. Boucher, staff photographer for the
Historic American Building Survey. Full photographic documentation of the Ryman Auditorium was
generously subsidized by the National Life and Accident Insurance Company, owners of the
building, with Albert Hutchison Jr., Chairman of the Historic Sites Federation of Tennessee, serving
as co-ordinator.

The measured drawings are by various architectural draftsmen employed by the National
Park Service.

John Kiser, Assistant Professor of Fine Arts, University of Tennessee at Nashville, supplied the
account of the Hays-Kiser house, in addition to working as a historian with HABS during the
second part of the Middle Tennessee survey.

The National Park Service's HABS researchers Professor Roy C. Pledger of Texas A. & M.,
Supervisory Architect, and Anatole Senkevitch Jr., Architectural Historian, in 1970 and 1971 recorded
most of the raw data on the buildings included here. With that as a basis, the text that accompanies
the pictures took form as a responsibility shared with me by Mr. Gore and by Vanderbilt University
Press's Martha I. Strayhorn, Editor. Mr. Gore then designed the handsome book which has
resulted from these various collaborations.

T. B. B.

Contents

Schools, Institutions

Residences

Architecture of Middle Tennessee

Tennessee State Capitol

BUILT more than a century ago, on the highest point in Nashville, the Tennessee State Capitol represents Greek-revival architecture at its finest. It is regarded as a masterwork of its designer, William F. Strickland of Philadelphia, leading architect of the mid-nineteenth century and outstanding exponent of the Greek revival in America.

The Capitol has been in continuous use since the legislature first met in it in 1853. Extensive restoration and repairs to remedy decades of neglect and to modernize the building for most efficient present-day use were completed in 1960.

The building site—Capitol Hill, on Charlotte Avenue between Sixth and Seventh avenues, North—was Cedar Knob, to early Tennesseans. In 1844, when the city of Nashville bought it from Judge G. W. Campbell for $30,000 and gave it to the state as a site for the Capitol, it was also called Campbell's Hill. A legislative act of October 7, 1843, had just made Nashville the permanent capital of Tennessee, ending years of fierce competition for that honor among several cities. Before 1843, the legislature had met at various places, including Knoxville, Kingston, Nashville, and Murfreesboro.

On January 30, 1844, another legislative act appointed a five-man board of commissioners to select an architect and supervise construction of the Capitol. Former Governor William Carroll was chairman. The commissioners, all Nashville businessmen, were William Nichol, John M. Bass, James Erwin, Morgan W. Brown, and Samuel D. Morgan. Morgan was the only man to remain on the board throughout the Capitol's construction; its completion as originally planned was largely his doing.

Unimpressed by building designs from several well-known architects, the board wrote to several others, including Strickland. Strickland had begun his career as apprentice to Benjamin Henry Latrobe, associate of Thomas Jefferson and one of the designers of the national Capitol in Washington. He had helped to organize and was the first president of the American Institution (later, Institute) of Architects.[1] Strickland's classic designs in Philadelphia—for the Bank of the United States (1824), restoration at Independence Hall (1828), the U.S. Mint (1829), the Merchants' Exchange (1834, showing an early use of the choragic-monument motif)—and various railroad and canal-engineering achievements had brought him fame and success before he was approached in 1844 by Tennessee's Board of Capitol Commissioners. He was highly qualified for the job, and he was interested. When he presented his plan for the building, with specifications and estimates, in Nashville on May 20, 1845, the board accepted it.

Strickland's estimated construction time was three years, and his figures on total cost were "$340,000 if done by contract," an amount that could be reduced to "$240,000 to $260,000"[2] if prison labor were used.

The legislative act creating the Board of Capitol Commissioners had also specified that funds for the project were to be available by legislative appropriation only and that prison labor was to be used, to keep costs as low as possible. These stipulations severely limited both commissioners and architect and made it impossible for the work to be completed within the bounds of Strickland's estimates.

The cornerstone was laid on July 4, 1845; but it was ten years before the final stone was put into place in the tower, and the terrace was not completed until 1859. There is no conclusive record of the total cost of the original building, but estimates place it between $900,000 and $1,500,000.[3]

The work proceeded piecemeal, held back by lack of skilled labor, problems in acquiring materials, and the need to request appropriations for continuation from successive legislatures. Opposition and criticism were constant.

1. Federal Writers' Project, *Tennessee: A Guide to the State*, p. 160.
2. Tennessee *Senate Journal*, 1845–1846, Appendix, pp. 55–56.
3. *Tennessee Blue Book*, 1963–1964, p. 197.

Lacy ironwork is suspended over austere Doric.

4   After nine years on the job, Strickland died, on April 6, 1854. The legislature directed that he be buried in a vault in the northeast wall of the north portico. S. D. Morgan, who assumed most of the responsibility for the building's completion after Strickland's death, is also buried in the Capitol—in the southeast corner of the south portico.

Strickland's son and assistant, Francis W. Strickland, was employed to continue the work after his father's death, but he was dismissed on May 1, 1857. He was succeeded by H. M. Akeroyed.

The Capitol follows the plan of an Ionic temple. The building is rectangular, 238 feet by 109 feet, including the porticoes on all four facades. It stands two stories tall, with a full basement. An 18-foot-wide flagged terrace surrounds it. The long gable roof is copper, supported by cast-iron rafters. From its center rises a Corinthian tower with a square base 42 feet tall, whose upper section, a 37-foot circular lantern or cupola, is a handsome variation on the choragic monument of Lysicrates in Athens. The top of the tower is crowned with iron foliated finial ornaments surmounted by a flagpole. The tower is supported by four massive piers, each measuring 10 feet by 12 feet.[4] The building's over-all height is 170 feet. Strickland's use of the tower instead of a dome was distinctive: forty U.S. state capitols have domes, instead.[5]

Strickland's plan for the building called for "a Doric basement" (ground floor) and "four Ionic porticos."[6] The porticos are modeled after those of the Erechtheum at Athens. Those at the ends of the building, facing north and south, have eight fluted columns with hand-carved capitals of solid stone. Those centered along the building's sides, facing east and west, have six columns. The twenty-eight columns, all 4 feet in diameter and 33 feet high,[7] carry appropriate entablatures of architrave, frieze, and cornice, with pediments at the ends and parapets at the side porticos.

Strickland intended the main entrance to be that on the long east side of the building. Since the south entrance, facing Charlotte Avenue, is the one nearest downtown Nashville, however, it has long been used as the main entrance.[8]

Fossilized limestone, quarried less than a mile west of the Capitol, was used for the foundation and walls. The foundation is 7 feet thick, to support the weight of the superstructure. Upper walls are 4½ feet thick. Enormous quantities of limestone were needed, since both exterior and interior walls were made of it, a practice unique at that time.[9] Interior columns of the legislative chambers and other decorative features inside were of marble from East Tennessee.

Prisoners from the old state penitentiary—at that time quite near the building site—and slaves rented for a monthly fee helped to quarry and cut the stone blocks, which were 4½ to 7 feet thick[10] and from 6 to 10 tons in weight. Strickland was able to hire enough skilled stone masons, setters, and cutters to insure excellent workmanship throughout: the stone blocks were so perfectly cut and so closely fitted that the average mortar joint is less than 3/16 of an inch.[11] The hewn stone was fitted into place in the walls with block and tackle and wooden derricks.[12]

The building's interior is handsomely proportioned, simply and efficiently planned. Floors and walls are of granite. The first and second floors are intersected by a central hall and

4. *The Official and Political Manual of the State of Tennessee*, pp. 2–3.

5. George E. Shankle, *State Names, Flags, Seals, Songs, Birds, Flowers, and Other Symbols* (New York: The H. W. Wilson Co., 1934), p. 294.

6. Tennessee *Senate Journal*, 1845–1846, Appendix, pp. 55–56.

7. *Official and Political Manual of the State of Tennessee*, p. 2.

8. Marilyn D. Franzen, editor, *Capital Capsules*, p. 172.

9. Nell Savage Mahoney, "William Strickland and the Building of Tennessee's Capitol, 1845–1854," p. 128.

10. Federal Writers' Project, *Tennessee: A Guide to the State*, p. 189.

11. Mahoney, p. 131; Wilbur F. Creighton, *Building of Nashville*, p. 107.

12. Mahoney, p 130; Creighton, p. 105.

State Capitol
Nashville

longitudinal hall which connects with stairways, porticos, offices, and principal chambers. The Greek-revival elements have been well adapted, so that classic orders and details do not hamper the total effect. In his later work, Strickland was more and more the purist, caring less and less for decorative detail.

Executive offices occupy the first floor. The marble staircase from first to second floor, centered in the west side, leads to a landing, then returns on both sides to the second floor. The second flights are of cut stone cantilevered from the walls of the central hall.

On the second floor are the Hall of Representatives, the Senate Chamber, and, directly opposite, an elegant room with frescoed ceiling and elaborately decorative cast-iron balcony and stair, originally the State Library. The room is modeled after the library of Sir Walter Scott in Abbotsford, Scotland.[13] It became the Legislative Lounge when the new State Library and Archives building was completed in 1954.

13. Mrs. John Trotwood Moore, "The Tennessee State Library in the Capitol," p. 8.

During the Civil War and for some seventy-five years thereafter, the Capitol deteriorated badly. The Tennessee limestone, which Strickland had praised lavishly, proved to be unusually friable, subject to excessive deterioration when exposed to moisture and weather changes. Seams of phosphate scattered

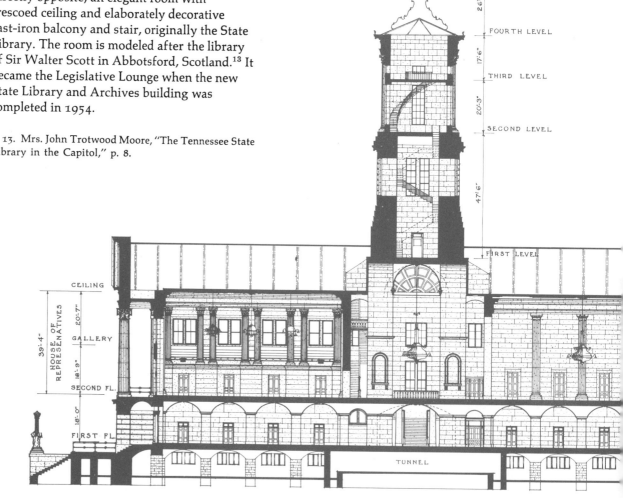

Longitudinal Section, West
Black areas indicate stone sections
HABS drawing by Richard R. Clark

throughout contributed to this: when water penetrated a seam and froze, segments of the stone were chipped off.[14]

By 1953, deterioration was far advanced. Funds were provided by the legislature for restoration and repair of the exterior. Work began in January 1956, to replace deteriorated

stone, install new windows, and put on a new copper roof—the original one had been replaced by a tin roof in 1885. Since building limestone is not commercially produced in Tennessee,[15] 90,000 cubic feet of Indiana limestone was used to rebuild the steps and terraces and replace the

14. Clayton B. Dekle, "The Tennessee State Capitol," p. 12.

15. *Ibid.*, p. 25.

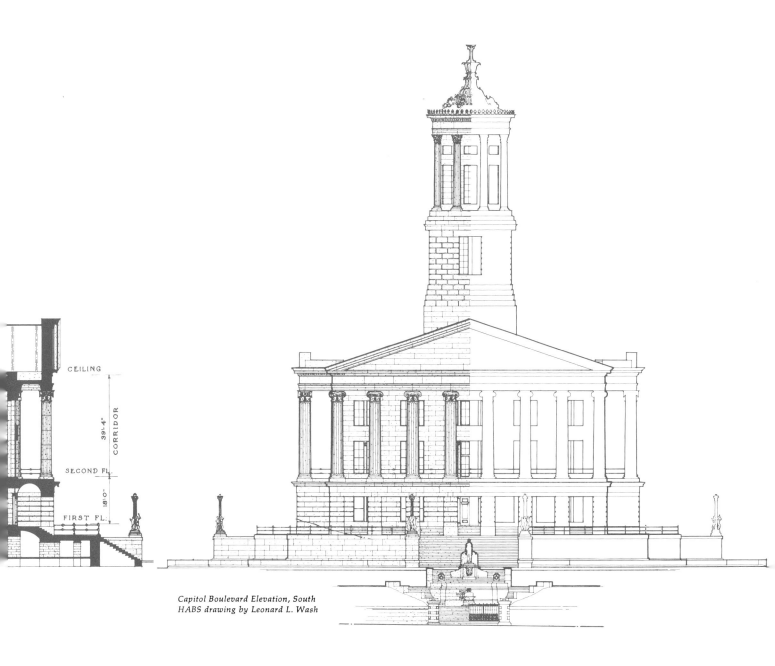

Capitol Boulevard Elevation, South
HABS drawing by Leonard L. Wash

State Capitol
Nashville

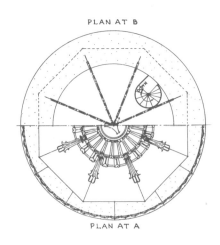

Just as Renaissance popes needed to see in miniature the buildings they commissioned, the Tennessee legislature was shown a model of the lantern—a detail of the fine new structure that they were about to erect.

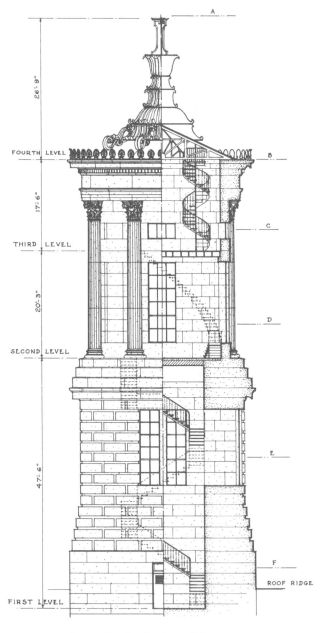

Lantern Elevation, Section, and Plan
HABS drawing

twenty-eight Ionic columns ornamenting the four porticoes, along with pediments, parapets, cornices, and entablatures.

Extensive restoration and repair of the interior began two years later. Limestone floors were replaced on the first and second levels with marble of a similar color from Carthage, Missouri, and in the restoration of ceilings in the legislative chambers, library, and corridors, earlier colors and styles were carefully matched.

The ground floor was excavated and finished, providing a great deal more office space. Complete new heating, air conditioning, and electrical systems were installed. A pedestrian tunnel was excavated from the north side of Charlotte Avenue, at street level, to the center of the Capitol, 13 feet below the foundation, and two elevators were installed.[16]

The grounds were also completely renovated and landscaped, and a new access road to the Capitol from Seventh Avenue, North, was constructed, abandoning the old approach from Sixth Avenue, North.

16. Creighton, p. 114.

Details of Portico Columns

Clayton, W. W. *History of Davidson County, Tennessee, with Illustrations and Biographical Sketches of Its Prominent Men.* Philadelphia: J. W. Lewis & Co., 1880.

Creighton, Wilbur F. *Building of Nashville.* Nashville: Wilbur F. Creighton Jr., 1969.

Dardis, George. *Description of the Plan, Structure, and Apartments of the State Capitol of Tennessee.* Nashville: G. C. Corbett, 1855.

Dekle, Clayton B. "The Tennessee State Capitol." *Tennessee Historical Quarterly* XXV (Fall 1966), 213–238.

Federal Writers' Project. *Tennessee: A Guide to the State.* New York: Viking Press, 1939.

Franzen, Marilyn D., editor. *Capital Capsules.* Pierpont, S.D.: Rushmore, Inc., 1964.

Gilchrist, Agnes A. *William Strickland, Architect and Engineer, 1788–1854.* Philadelphia: University of Pennsylvania Press, 1950.

Mahoney, Nell Savage. "William Strickland and the Building of Tennessee's Capitol, 1845–1854." *Tennessee Historical Quarterly*, IV (June 1945), 99–153.

Moore, Mrs. John Trotwood. "The Tennessee State Library in the Capitol. *Tennessee Historical Quarterly*, XII (March 1953), 3–22.

Nashville, Tennessee. Nashville Public Library. Restoration and Repair, Tennessee State Capitol. Photographs made during the restoration of the Capitol Building, March 1956 to January 1959. Photographs by Charles W. Warterfield. 2 vols.

Official and Political Manual of the State of Tennessee. Prepared by Charles A. Miller. Nashville: Marshall and Bruce, Stationers, 1890.

Roberts, Charles E. *Nashville and Her Trade for 1870.* Nashville: Roberts & Purvis, 1870.

Wooldridge, John, editor. *History of Nashville, Tennessee.* Nashville: H. W. Crew, 1890.

Tennessee State Penitentiary

THE Tennessee State Penitentiary stands at the western end of Nashville's Centennial Boulevard, seven miles west of the Davidson County Courthouse. The conical roofs and graceful turrets of its Administration Building, which first meets the eye, look surprisingly like a French chateau set on the south bank of the Cumberland River.

This is the third state penitentiary built in Nashville. Its predecessors, constructed in 1831 and 1858, both stood within sight of the Capitol—approximately where Sixteenth Avenue, North, now crosses Church Street and Charlotte Avenue, a mile or so southwest of the courthouse.

A maximum security prison,[1] the State Penitentiary is the main unit of the state's penal system. When it was built, between 1895 and 1897, it was considered one of the most modern and humane prisons in the United States.

S. M. Patton, a Chattanooga architect, designed the penitentiary. Patton was the second architect on the job. When the Tennessee legislature in 1893 authorized a new prison to be built, the contract was awarded to J. P. Fulcher and Company, with William C. Smith as architect. The cost was not to exceed $600,000. Soon afterward, an investigating committee of the legislature found that the Fulcher contract was in excess of the costs imposed by the authorizing bill. Amid charges of collusion and political favoritism, the contract was abrogated. A new contract was awarded on October 26, 1895, to H. H. Squair and Company, of Rockwood, Tennessee, and Patton was retained as architect. It was according to his designs that the State Penitentiary was built.

A point which Patton stressed in his first annual report to the legislators was that the penitentiary was built almost entirely of materials native to Tennessee. "It is estimated that not over twenty percent of the total cost of the new Penitentiary and its appurtenances were spent for materials outside of the State of Tennessee," he noted.

All of the brick, common and pressed, were made on the State Farm. All the stone for the walls was quarried in Middle and East Tennessee. Vitrified brick, used in the construction of the cells, were manufactured at Robbins, Scott County, Tennessee. The cast and malleable iron work was made in Nashville and Chattanooga. All the sanitary pipe was manufactured at South Pittsburg. The doors, sashes, etc., were made in Nashville. The boilers, fireplace arches, ceilings, etc., were made in Chattanooga. Wherever practical, preference was given to home manufacturers. A large portion of soft steel work was changed to malleable iron when it was found that the latter could be furnished at the same price, would answer the purpose equally well, and could be made out of Tennessee iron by Tennessee foundries.[2]

The prison complex consists of approximately fifty separate buildings[3] enclosed in 20-foot walls of stone and concrete. It occupies approximately 154 acres[4] of the 3600-acre State Penitentiary tract in Cockrill Bend that the state now owns. Originally, the site consisted of 1,128 acres bought in 1894.

Most of the main buildings were erected before 1900. They include the Administration Building, the Main Prison—a group of buildings forming the south side of the enclosure, consisting of the central cell block and the east and west wings—hospital, dining hall, classification and maximum security buildings, and various utility, industry, and classroom buildings.

Construction is brick and concrete throughout. The foundations, of rockfaced Tennessee limestone, are in some places as much as five feet deep and the average thickness of

1. Tennessee State Planning Commission, *A Plan for the Disposal and Industrial Development of the Tennessee State Prison Farm Area*, p. 2.

2. Tennessee Board of Prison Commissioners, *Report*, 1st–10th, 1895/96–1913/14, First Annual Report of the Architect, S. M. Patton, to the Tennessee Legislature, 1896, p. 10.

3. Tennessee State Planning Commission, *A Study of the State Institutions*, Bulletin No. 5-E: *Tennessee State Penitentiary at Nashville*, p. 1.

4. Tennessee State Planning Commission, *A Plan for the Disposal and Industrial Development of the Tennessee State Prison Farm Area*, p. 2.

State Penitentiary
Nashville

The flood of light that security demands for an antiquated structure shows the central core as a fantasy castle set against grim cell blocks.

State Penitentiary
Nashville

14 the wall is about 2 feet 6 inches.

Originally, the Women's Prison was in a red brick building in a corner of the Main Prison compound. In 1965, after its having been recommended for many years, the Women's Prison was moved to a modern plant near Jordonia, outside the penitentiary walls.

Centered directly in front and outside the walls, the four-story Administration Building, with its towers, turrets, and dormers, dominates the area. The structure is built of white brick, fireproof, and it stands four stories tall with basement. It contains administrative offices, the chapel, the warden's quarters, and the main guardroom and arsenal. The entry hall contains the stairway and provides access to the cell blocks through an open balcony 16 feet wide above the first floor. A cross-hall opens into offices and storage rooms. There are stoops at the main entrance and side entrances at either end of the cross-hall. The roof is steeply pitched, of galvanized iron with standing seams on circular sawn wood. Turrets appear at each corner, and there are four dormers. General repairs over the years have included rebuilding the central tower over the main hall and mending or replacing roofs on the various buildings.[5] Many of the original ornate brass door knobs and lock plates remain.

A new chapel was completed in 1963, with furnishings built at the prison shops.

The central cell block, directly behind the Administration Building, and the east and west wings make a total frontage of 700 feet. These buildings, of concrete, brick, and stone, are 55 feet high. The block contains 800 cells; five walks of eighty cells each make up each 320-foot wing.

5. Tennessee Department of Institutions, Departmental Report, Tennessee State Library and Archives, Record Group No. 11, Series No. 23, Box No. 24.

Behind the theatrical effect of the roof line is a chaotic world of metal struts and braces.

BIBLIOGRAPHY

Nashville, Tennessee. Research and Development
Division, Tennessee State Penitentiary. "A History of
the Tennessee State Prison" [by Norman Lee].

Tennessee Board of Prison Commissioners. *Report*,
1st–10th, 1895/96–1913/14. Nashville, 1896–1915.

Tennessee State Penitentiary. Nashville. *Biennial Report
of the Warden to the Board of Prison Commissioners
for 1897–1898.* Nashville: Brandon Printing Company,
1899.

Tennessee State Planning Commission. *A Plan for the
Disposal and Industrial Development of the Tennessee
State Prison Farm Area.* [Prepared by Otis Trimble.]
Nashville: State Planning Commission, 1958.

Tennessee State Planning Commission. *A Study of State
Institutions.* Bulletin Series, No. 5-E, January 1937

Federal Building
(Old Clarksville Post Office)

THE Old Clarksville Post Office—now the Federal Building—is a square one-story brick structure facing east at the corner of Commerce and South Second streets in Clarksville, Montgomery County.

Erected between 1897 and 1898 to serve as a post office, the building is relatively small—62 feet 2 inches square—but unusually flamboyant in style for its size. Its design is unique in Tennessee. Its highly pitched roof, with large eagles on the four corners, its steeply gabled windows and elaborate terra-cotta ornamentation contribute to its original appearance.

The lot on which the Federal Building stands was bought for $6,135.41 by the U.S. government on May 26, 1894. Appropriations for its construction were made by Congressional Acts of August 5, 1892, March 3, 1893, and March 2, 1895. The building cost $43,033.96. In 1936, the property was sold to the City of Clarksville, the present owner. The building is now occupied by the Clarksville Department of Electricity.

The building's foundations are of smooth stone. Exterior walls are natural brick with decorative terra cotta around all openings and on the corners. The hipped roof with flared eaves has steel framing and was covered with slate. Inside, special decorative features are the extensive natural white-oak trim and the marble floors. Originally, there was an elaborate coffered plaster ceiling, now covered by false ceilings installed by the Department of Electricity in 1938 in all areas of the main floor except the entrance lobby.

William Martin Aiken, supervising architect of the United States Treasury from 1895 to 1897, designed the Federal Building. Its construction was supervised by David A. Murphy, a builder who, before coming to Clarksville, had served in Ohio, Kentucky, and Texas as Superintendent of Construction for United States government buildings, a post to which he was appointed by President William McKinley, for whom he had written a campaign song.

BIBLIOGRAPHY

Clarksville *Daily Leaf-Chronicle*, August 6, 1897.
Clarksville *Daily Leaf-Chronicle*, November 1, 1898.
Clarksville *Leaf Chronicle* (semiweekly), December 3, 1897.
Washington, D.C. General Services Administration. Public Buildings Service.

Patriotic eagles guard the cardinal points of an extraordinary roof line.

Federal Building
Clarksville

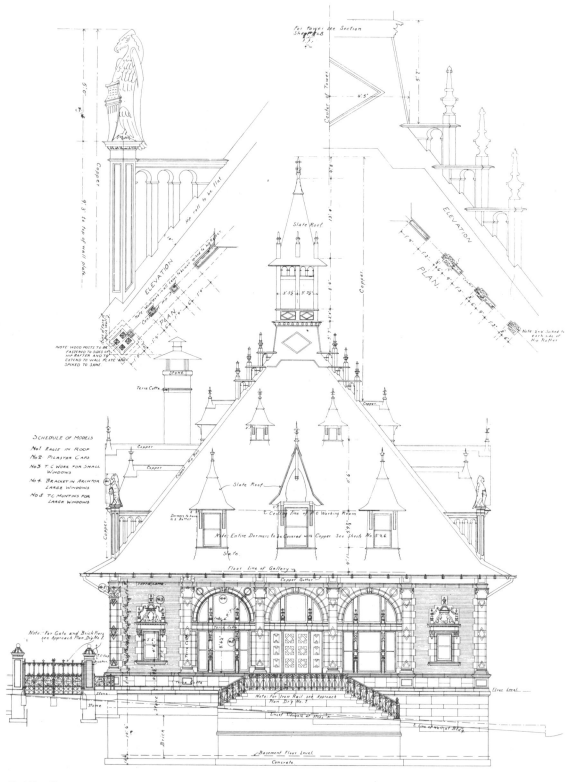

East Elevation
Architect's drawing dated 5-6-1897

The delicate effect of the east-elevation drawing is scarcely changed by its execution in terra cotta.

The Poston Buildings

THE Poston Buildings in Clarksville are Nos. 126, 128, and 130 Main Street, at the southwest corner of the intersection of Main and Telegraph streets—the Public Square.

This block of three buildings is the oldest surviving structure used for business purposes in Montgomery County. The buildings show a remarkable resemblance to Philadelphia stores of the mid-nineteenth century. The similarity may be due to Philadelphia business connections developed by John H. Poston, the merchant for whom the structures were built on Lot No. 57, about 1843.

Poston went to Clarksville in 1805, when he was nineteen, as a young merchant acting for William King. When King died in 1808, Poston was a partner in his large estate in Tennessee. Active in civic, financial, church, and political affairs, Poston became, successively, a militia officer, alderman, commissioner of the Red River Bridge Company, and a member of the group chartering the Clarksville Male Academy in 1820 and the Clarksville Female Academy sixteen years later. In 1830, he was elected mayor of Clarksville, and in 1836, postmaster. He was the founder-president of the Branch Bank of Tennessee in Clarksville in 1835 and was also the founder of the Clarksville Marine Insurance and Trust Company.

A deed dated September 7, 1843, conveying land at the northwest corner of the Public Square, Lot No. 57, from John H. Poston to John F. Couts and Adeline Poston Couts—Poston's son-in-law and daughter—refers to the "block of buildings lately erected by John H. Poston." In the corner building of the block, No. 130, Couts opened a grocery store which he operated there for two years before converting it to a furniture store and undertaking establishment. A large sign dating from around 1870, advertising Couts's furniture and undertaking business, is still visible, painted on the end wall of the block so that it might be seen by river traffic.

The rectangular-shaped block faces east, extending 59 feet 7 inches on Main Street and running back 45 feet. Foundations are of Tennessee limestone, and the walls are English-

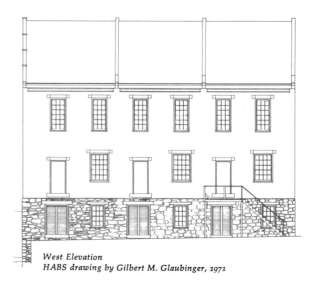

West Elevation
HABS drawing by Gilbert M. Glaubinger, 1971

bonded brick. The buildings are two stories high, with full basements. There are five brick chimneys, and the roof, at its north end, retains a stepped gable. The buildings appear to have changed little, being of the same plan and construction today as when they were built.

Inside, the three are connected by interior doors. Each building contains stairs leading to the second level and the basement. There is recent hardwood flooring laid on hand-hewn floor joists. The average joist is 11 inches by 3 inches, 20 inches on center.

In November 1973, fire damaged approximately a third of the two-story Poston block, making the future of the historic structures uncertain. Until they were damaged by the fire, Buildings 126 and 128 had been used for storage by the Torino Cigar Manufacturing Company for the past several years. No. 130 is unoccupied except for a basement room used as a plumber's repair shop.

BIBLIOGRAPHY

Beach, Ursula Smith. *Along the Warioto*. Nashville: McQuiddy Press, 1964.

Tennessee. Montgomery County. Register of Deeds.

Titus, William P. *Picturesque Clarksville, Past and Present*. Clarksville: William P. Titus, 1887.

Uneeda Biscuits are still advertised at five cents a box to a greatly diminished river traffic.

S. D. Morgan & Company

(*Now J. S. Reeves & Company Building*)

IN what the Nashville *Union and American* called "by far the most disastrous conflagration that has ever visited Nashville,"[1] a series of fires struck Nashville's Public Square and the surrounding area in the spring and summer of 1856, destroying the courthouse, the Nashville Inn, and a number of wholesale houses and warehouses on the Square's north side.

One of the first structures to go up around the Square after the rubble was cleared that year was a wholesale dry goods store built by Samuel D. Morgan. Though much of the distinction that S. D. Morgan achieved as a business and civic leader in Nashville has been obscured by time, he was, in the last half of the nineteenth century, one of the area's most promising and successful merchants. Establishing the firm of Morgan, Crutcher and Company in 1837, he helped to found Nashville's wholesale dry goods trade. In 1836 or 1837, he built, in Lebanon, the first cotton mill in Middle Tennessee, possibly the first in the state. During the Civil War, he helped to produce munitions for the Confederacy, and the gun-cap factory which he built in South Nashville made the caps first fired at the Battle of Manassas.[2] Just after the Civil War, Morgan helped to plan and build the Tennessee Manufacturing Company, one of the best-constructed mills in the South.[3] He is credited with writing the charter of the first railroad in Tennessee, the Nashville and Chattanooga, which served as a model for all subsequent charters.

Probably Morgan's most distinguished work, however, was as chairman of the State Capitol Building Committee. It was largely through Morgan's efforts that William Strickland's design for the Tennessee State Capitol was chosen over alternate designs, and he supported Strickland's recommendations throughout the Capitol's construction. It was through Morgan's efforts that the State Library was equipped and the grounds graded and landscaped. In appreciation of his services, the legislature directed that Morgan be interred in a niche in the south wall of the Capitol.

In view of his distinguished background in architecture and business, it is not surprising that Samuel Morgan should have erected a building of architectural distinction for his business.

The S. D. Morgan & Company building is a fine example of the richly decorated Italianate store-front. It was erected at 208–210 Public Square in 1856, and it may show the first significant use of cast-iron elements in commercial buildings in the Nashville area. These consist of columns positioned on a regular structural grid on the first, second, and third floors, as well as the first-story store-front, with its unusual hinged side panels on each of the pilasters. The building stands on land bought in 1853 by Morgan & Company, made up of Samuel D. Morgan and partners R. H. Gardner, C. J. Cluney, and R. C. Gardner. In 1857, Morgan bought out his partners.

The four-story building, known during Morgan's ownership as Number Forty-nine, faces south, extending 41 feet along the Public Square and running back from the street some 180 feet. The solid masonry walls are 30 inches thick, on stone foundations. One brick chimney remains of the original four that served the four wood-burning fireplaces first used to heat each floor. The structural system is post and beam. Interior supports are cast-iron columns with Corinthian capitals. The raked stone cornices are supported by Corinthian brackets.

At Morgan's death in 1880, the Chancery Court ordered the sale of his storehouse "for [not] less than $20,000" and it was purchased in 1882 by Mary F. Frouillary. It was bought by the Reeves family on February 6, 1897, when John P. and Anne F. White sold it to Joe E. Reeves. The building remained under the ownership of the J .S. Reeves Company until its sale in August of 1963 to the agents for the Washington Manufacturing Company. It is still in use as a dry goods store.

---

1. April 14, 1856.
2. E. C. Lewis, "Nashville's Pre-Eminent Merchant and Manufacturer," p. 19.
3. J. Wooldridge, editor, *History of Nashville, Tennessee*, p. 628.

The Morgan Building was an integral part of the architectural ensemble of appealing interrelationships once displayed on Nashville's Public Square.

S. D. Morgan and Co.
Nashville

24

South Elevation
HABS drawing by Robert J. Dunay, 1970

BIBLIOGRAPHY

Jones, Ira P. "The Dry Goods Market." In *The City of Nashville, Illustrated*, by Ira P. Jones, p. 77. Nashville: Ira P. Jones, 1890.

Lewis, E. C. "Nashville's Pre-eminent Merchant and Manufacturer." *The Merchant and Manufacturer*, XX, No. 7 (July 1914), 19, 43, 48.

Morrison, Andrew. "J. S. Reeves & Co." In *The City of Nashville*, by Andrew Morrison, p. 105. The Englehart Series: American Cities, XXIV. Nashville: n.p., 1891[?]

Nashville, Tennessee. Tennessee State Library and Archives. Manuscript Division. Ref. Ac. No. 67–138.

"Morgan [A Genealogy]."

Nashville, Tennessee. Tennessee State Library and Archives. Manuscript Division. Ac. No. 1081. "The Public Square," by Joe S. Reeves.

Reeves, J. S., & Company. "J. S. Reeves & Company." In *Glimpses of Nashville, Tennessee*, by J. S. Reeves & Co. Nashville: E. W. Softley, 1901[?]

Tennessee. Davidson County. County Clerk's Office.

Tennessee. Davidson County. Register's Office.

Wooldridge, John, editor. *History of Nashville, Tennessee*. Nashville: H. W. Crew, 1890.

Inside, the need for function and practicality determined a new aesthetic.

The Grange Warehouse

THE Grange Warehouse fronts on Riverside Drive between Adams and Washington streets, 300 feet from the east bank of the Cumberland River, in Clarksville, Montgomery County.

From 1876 until World War I, the Grange was the largest tobacco warehouse in the world, occupying an entire block on the river front. It is still among the largest existing brick tobacco warehouses, and may still be the world's largest. Measuring 279 by 246 feet and standing two stories high, with a partial third story, it covers some three acres of ground. The building has two distinct parts: the section fronting on Adams Street is called the Upper Grange, and the section fronting on Washington Street is the Lower Grange. They were often leased to different firms.

During its heyday, the Grange Warehouse's goods were shipped from its own wharf on the Cumberland River by boat to New Orleans and from there to foreign markets.

The Grange was built in 1858 or 1859 by William M. McReynolds and James M. Swift for use as a planing mill. It was later purchased by the Grange Warehouse Association. Evidently between 1887 and 1895, the structure was greatly enlarged so that the Upper Grange contained three levels, and the Lower Grange two, its capacity in 1887 being described as 3,000 hogsheads, while it is described as 10,000 hogsheads in 1895. Because it was built on an incline, external access is provided to each of the warehouse's three floors.

Early settlers of Montgomery County, from North Carolina and Virginia, were familiar with methods of culture and curing of tobacco, which was grown in the area before the county was named. The tobacco produced in the Clarksville area was a dark, heavy leaf similar to that produced in the James River area of Virginia and was much sought after in Europe. In 1820, 7,000 hogsheads were shipped to New Orleans each year for foreign markets. In 1895, Clarksville had become the largest export center for tobacco in the United States, as well as being the country's third largest tobacco market. Shipments of up to 40,000 hogsheads a year went from Clarksville to Germany, France, Italy, Austria, Spain, and Africa. The tobacco market has since declined, but Clarksville is still an important local market.

The Grange Warehouse has brick foundations and load-bearing masonry walls with wood truss. The joists are exposed on the interior, as shown.

The warehouse is now used to store tobacco during tobacco season and as a storage warehouse for Rudolph Transfer and Storage Company, a moving company.

BIBLIOGRAPHY

Beach, Ursula S. *Along the Warioto.* Nashville: McQuiddy Press, 1964.

History of Tennessee. Nashville: The Goodspeed Publishing Co., 1886.

The National Trade Review, Clarksville Edition. Evansville, Indiana: Keller Printing Co., May 1895.

Tennessee. Montgomery County. Register's Office.

Titus, William P. *Picturesque Clarksville, Past and Present.* Clarksville: William P. Titus, 1887.

Here, timeless building methods provide the vast space originally needed to store the annual tobacco crop.

Second Avenue, North
Commercial District

NASHVILLE'S commercial district includes a
long block of warehouses fronting on
Second Avenue, North, and extending northward
from Broadway to Church Street. The
block-deep buildings run back, eastward,
lengthwise, all the way to First Avenue, North.
Apparently, freight and merchandise were
loaded through the rear façades on First
Avenue, directly from the city wharf on the
Cumberland River just across the street.

Initially known as Market Street, this Second
Avenue segment of Nashville's commercial
district from Broadway to the Public Square
was probably the most important business
street in the city in the last half of the
nineteenth century. It housed the principal
wholesale district, less than a block west of the
Cumberland River. The city wharf, at Broadway
and First Avenue, was a transportation center
during much of the nineteenth century, when
most of the city's freight was shipped by boat
down the Cumberland. Easy access to shipping
facilities explains in great part the wholesale
district's location so close to the river. In the
early 1900s, with railroads crossing the state,
water transportation almost ceased; but river
traffic grew active again on barges and tugboats
in the 1930s.

The eastern segment of Second Avenue between
Church Street and Broadway is the only part
of the nineteenth-century streetscape to survive
substantially intact. Its store-fronts have been
uncommonly well preserved. This remarkable
row of exuberant store-fronts maintains the
lively texture of Nashville's cityscape in the
last quarter of the nineteenth century. The
buildings are presently in use as warehouses,
retail outlets, and offices.

The buildings are of high quality and uniform
scale, averaging between 30 and 50 feet in
width and varying from 3 to 5 stories high.
Outside of the East Coast, this is one of the
more remarkable groupings of nineteenth-century
commercial buildings to be found in the United
States, and every effort should be made to
insure its preservation.

Little is known of the precise evolution of
buildings on Market Street. A map, "Nashville
in 1854," unidentified as to source or publisher[1]
indicates for that year a solid row of buildings
along Market Street between Broad and the
Public Square. The buildings are not continuous
from Market to Front streets, as they are today,
but are shown as peripheral structures around
the ends of the blocks, with the center portions
devoid of buildings.

Charles E. Roberts, in his *Nashville and Her
Trade for 1870*, suggests that construction of the
buildings surviving today was begun in 1869.
He speaks of "four- and five-story [business]
houses, elaborately ornamented and beautified,
and rich and costly in their designs," and
mentions specifically one block of buildings on
the east side of Market Street, erected in 1869,
which still stands: "the Spring Brook Block
[erected] at [a cost of] $140,000" (p. 50).

The principal façades of the Second Avenue
buildings, on the whole, employed cast-iron
fronts for the ground floor only. These one-story
cast-iron fronts usually were crowned by a
cornice scaled to the ground floor. The treatment
of the façade from the second through the
third, fourth, or fifth story, depending on the
height of the building, was either plain wall
surface or a surface articulated by pilasters;
richly treated window frames were customary
in both instances, as were elaborate cornices
surmounting the façade and scaled for the entire
building. Special decorative features included
ornate cast-iron window pediments and very
detailed, intricate patterns in brick and in
terra cotta on exterior walls. Foundations are of
random ashlar rock-face Tennessee limestone.

Brief comments on some of the principal
buildings follow, with references to lot
numbers shown on maps located in the
Metropolitan Nashville Courthouse.

The building on lot 15 is a three-story brick, a

1. Item 409, Photographic File, Library Division,
Tennessee State Library and Achives, Nashville,
Tennessee.

PHIL
PAINT

S & QUARLES HAR

DO NOT
ENTER

LEASE

OPEN

30 6-bay edifice which appears to have been erected at the turn of the twentieth century.

The building which now occupies lot 18 is clearly a product of the twentieth century.

The two buildings on lots 19 and 20 are noted on an engraving of Second Avenue entitled "Market Street—from Church, South," by the Moss Engraving Company, dating from the 1890s.[2] The cast-iron fronts on both buildings today remain surprisingly intact and devoid of modern embellishments. The identical crowning cornices provide a handsome touch.

According to the inscription it bears, the Rhea Building on lot 67 was erected in 1887.

The building occupying lots 69–71 belongs to the Spring Brook Buildings mentioned earlier. It is very likely the earliest of the buildings in the row. A three-story structure, its architectural treatment is rather simple but still decidedly Italianate. It has a cast-iron front on the ground floor.

The group of buildings on lots 72–74 adjoining those to the south are obviously a block. No date is known for their construction, but the handsome grouping of three-story, four-window-wide façades suggests a transition from the Italianate. A construction date in the early 1870s is likely.

A stone set into the central pilaster of the building on lot 75 reads "Pilcher." The general modernistic design of the façade suggests a date somewhere in the 1920s or 1930s.

Nothing is known of the building on lot 76, but its division of the façade into two two-window-wide segments and the treatment of its window pediments suggests the late phase of the Italianate which appeared in Nashville during the last two decades of the nineteenth century.

The building occupying lot 77, a four-story, two-part store-front, is transitional between the nineteenth- and twentieth-century styles. The severity of its lines, the large window openings, and the simplification of the crowning cornice all speak of influences of the Chicago School of commercial architecture which appear to have come to Nashville at the turn of the century.

In contrast, the handsome three-story building to the south on lot 78 is clearly indicative of buildings in Nashville dating from the early 1880s. The brick work in this building is outstanding.

The buildings on lots 79, 81, and 82 all represent attempts in the 1920s to erect modernistic buildings somewhat compatible with their striking nineteenth-century neighbors. The building on lot 79 is inscribed "Hooper—1924."

Set in the middle of these modernistic variants is an exquisite three-story tripartite store-front which exemplifies early commercial architecture in Nashville. The attic over the cornice carries the date 1879. This building shows the strong vertical proportions, rich surface treatment, and the exaggerated profiles of the prototype nineteenth-century commercial structure in Nashville.

Lots 83–86 make up the "Watkins Block," whose buildings provide the date 1875. It seems to combine the modest simplicity of the Spring Brook Buildings with the more elaborate treatment of the block on lots 72–74 immediately to the south.

Lots 87–88 and 90–96 contain no permanent buildings.

On the corner of Broadway and Second Avenue, on lot 89, stands the lone survivor of the buildings which once stood at the southern end of the commercial district. Once the Silver Dollar saloon, this handsome three-story building was designed with an octagonal turret on the corner. It probably dates from the latter part of the nineteenth century.

2. Published in *Nashville: An Illustrated Review of Its Progress and Importance*, edited by John Cornman p. 13.

Despite varied ornament on individual structures, the nineteenth-century streetscape maintains a feeling of unity.

Second Avenue, North
Nashville

32   BIBLIOGRAPHY

Clayton, W. W. *History of Davidson County, Tennessee,
with Illustrations and Biographical Sketches of its
Prominent Men.* Philadelphia: J. W. Lewis & Co., 1880.

Criddle, Smith. "Map of the City of Nashville."
Surveyed by Smith Criddle, Cincinnati. Engraved by
Doolittle and Munson. Published by J. P. Ayres, 1831.

Federal Writers' Project. *Tennessee: A Guide to the
State.* New York: Viking Press, 1939.

Hopkins, G. M. *Atlas of the City of Nashville, Tennessee,
from Official Records, Private Plans, and Actual
Surveys.* Philadelphia: G. M. Hopkins, 1889.

Jones, Ira P. *The City of Nashville, Illustrated.* Nashville:
Ira P. Jones, 1890.

Morrison, Andrew. *The City of Nashville.* The Englehart
Series: American Cities, XXIV. Nashville: n.p., 1891[?].

*Nashville: An Illustrated Review of its Progress and
Importance.* Compiled and edited by John Cornman.
Nashville [?]: Enterprise Publishing Company, n.d.

Nashville, Tennessee. Tennessee State Library and
Archives. Tennessee Historical Society File, Item 409.
"Nashville in 1854."

Nashville, Tennessee. Tennessee State Library and
Archives. Library Division. Photographic File.

*Real Estate Atlas of Davidson County, Tennessee:
Detail Tax Maps.* 4th edition. Miami: Real Estate
Directories, 1970.

Roberts, Charles E. *Nashville and Her Trade for 1870.*
Nashville: Roberts & Purvis, 1870.

Waller, William, editor. *Nashville in the 1890s.*
Nashville: Vanderbilt University Press, 1970.

Wooldridge, John, editor. *History of Nashville,
Tennessee.* Nashville: H. W. Crew, 1890.

A surrealistic sign momentarily unsettles the commercial world around it.

Werthan Bag Corporation

(Formerly Tennessee Manufacturing Company)

34 ALTHOUGH it has been adapted to modern use and extended in size during the present century, the Werthan Bag Corporation building is the largest surviving nineteenth-century factory in the Middle Tennessee area.

The factory is actually a complex of buildings erected on Eighth Avenue, North, in Nashville, between 1871 and the late 1880s. The first section of the former Tennessee Manufacturing Company was built entirely of pressed brick which has since darkened to a red-gray color, adding to its austere and monumental aspect. According to Clayton's *History*, contracts for the main structure were

> entered into on January 1, 1870, and the work of building carried forward so rapidly under the immediate supervision of the president [Samuel D. Morgan] and executive committee, that a brick mill building was presented to the stockholders August 3, 1871, nearly complete, four stories high, besides the basement, with all the necessary outbuildings for the accommodation of 13,820 spindles, 400 looms, and its attendant preparatory and finishing machinery. One hundred and fifty looms and 7,500 spindles were immediately put in operation. The power was furnished by two 200-horse-power steam-engines. This was considered by practical men of the East as a model mill. With a paid-up capital of over $300,000, operations were commenced before January 1, 1872, manufacturing standard sheetings, drills, and shirtings. These goods were most favorably received by the trade, and at once were placed in the front rank among the various brands of cotton goods manufactured in the United States.[1]

Employment was given to "202 female and 66 male operatives at an average price of about $5 each per week," and the company was proud to report that it did not have to reduce wages during the gold panic.[2]

The main building, which faces Eighth Avenue, North, is reminiscent of the Tower of London, with four square "Norman" towers at its corners. Decorative corbeling just beneath the entablature is used to tie the eye around the structure. The fenestration is undistinguished but unusually plentiful throughout the various buildings. A large amount of natural light was thus provided for the interior working space.

A number of decorative and functional towers are introduced into the fabric of the main and subsidiary structures. In the warehouse section, a small four-story tower, dated 1881, is of the square Italian-villa type so popular in private residences of a decade or two earlier. It is decorated with arcading, quoined corners, a slender string course of white stone between the third and fourth stories, and there are tastefully designed architraves surmounting the windows and doors.

BIBLIOGRAPHY

Clayton, W. W. *History of Davidson County, Tennessee, with Illustrations and Biographical Sketches of Its Prominent Men.* Philadelphia: J. W. Lewis & Co., 1880.

1. W. W. Clayton, *History of Davidson County, Tennessee*, p. 222.
2. *Ibid.*

Werthan Bag Corporation
Nashville

Bricked-up windows, cyclone fence, and the innumerable accretions of a century are elements of industrial growth.

Bear Spring Furnace

BEAR SPRING FURNACE is in the Tennessee Ridge area near the Cumberland River, a little more than five miles east of Dover, on Highway 49 in Stewart County, Tennessee. Tennessee Ridge is the watershed between the Tennessee and Cumberland rivers.

This 37-foot-tall square limestone stack is all that is left of the charcoal coal-blast furnaces which brought Tennessee fifth rank in the nation in iron production during the last quarter of the nineteenth century.

The first furnace on this site was built by Joseph and Robert Woods and Thomas Yeatman in 1830; it was destroyed by Union forces in 1862, and the present furnace was built on the site in 1873. It remained in blast until 1907. Like the old furnace, this one used the high-grade brown hematite ore found locally, and fuel was provided by the surrounding 63,000 acres of timber. Water power was also used in its operation. A deposit of fire-clay of good quality, found near Dover, was used to line the furnaces.

The stack is 37 feet high, 38 feet square at the base, and 25 feet square at the top. The hearth is 6 feet 4 inches high. The entire structure was built of rusticated ashlar Tennessee limestone, laid without mortar. The battered walls have small openings on all four sides, over which steel lintels were placed. A special decorative feature is a stone carved in low relief over the north opening, which includes a primitive depiction of a bear, the words "Creek Spring Furnace," and the name of the architect, Ran Umbenhour.

The furnace is of the cold-blast type and was blown by an Arnslie and Cochran horizontal steam engine, generating some 3 ½ pounds of blast. The product of the furnace was rated at 14 ¾ tons per day, and 150 bushels of coal were consumed per ton. Production reached 17 tons, on occasion. In 1881, production costs for the furnace were listed as follows:

2 tons of ore [at] $2.00	$4.00
150 bushels charcoal [at] .07	10.50
Limestone	.50
Labor	2.46
	$17.46

The unusually large yield of this furnace was attributed to the richness of the ore and the great volume of blast from the engines. In 1901, the Dover Iron Company assumed ownership of the furnace, and a railroad was built to Tennessee Ridge at a cost of $100,000. The railroad is no longer there, and Highway 49 follows its bed. Operations at Bear Spring ceased in 1907.

BIBLIOGRAPHY

Killebrew, J. B. *Iron and Coal of Tennessee*. Nashville: Tavel and Howell, 1881.

Killebrew, J. B. *Introduction to the Resources of Tennessee*. Nashville: Tavel, Eastman, and Howell, 1874.

Nashville, Tennessee. Tennessee State Library and Archives. "A History of Stewart County," by Iris Hopkins McClain.

Tennessee. Stewart County. Office of the Register.

The Ryman Auditorium

THE red brick bulk of the Ryman Auditorium at 116 Opry Place (116 Fifth Avenue, North) occupies a quarter of a block in downtown Nashville. It was originally called the Union Gospel Tabernacle and was renamed the Ryman Auditorium in 1904, in honor of Captain Thomas Green Ryman, who perhaps did more to make the building a reality than did any other individual. Since 1941, the Ryman has been the home stage of Nashville radio station WSM's Saturday night country music show, the Grand Ole Opry. As a result, the big auditorium has been familiarly known, for a long time, as the Grand Ole Opry House—a name that became official in 1963, when the building was bought by the National Life and Accident Insurance Company, of which WSM is a subsidiary.

The deteriorating downtown area where the Ryman stands is also the city's most interesting and architecturally significant district. The five blocks from Opry Place to the Cumberland River contain the most important late-nineteenth-century commercial properties —warehouses and stores—which still survive in Nashville.[1] Itself a combination of both architectural and cultural history, the Ryman was placed on the National Register of Historic Places in 1971.

Although it was not built to serve either as an opera house or as a legitimate theater, the Ryman, with its excellent acoustics and one of the biggest stages in show business, has, through the years, presented one of the country's most distinguished rosters in the performing arts and has earned a national reputation.

The idea for the auditorium took shape in 1885. Construction began in 1888, and the building was completed in 1892, at an estimated cost of $100,000. Contributions from citizens of Nashville paid part of the building cost; part of it came through fund-raising committees; part came from the continuing efforts of Captain

Ryman and the Reverend Sam Jones.

Ryman was a riverboat captain, owner of several steam packets whose operation along the Cumberland River had made him wealthy. Jones was a professional revivalist whose great influence and large following throughout the South drew enormous crowds to his powerful, emotion-packed sermons. In May 1885, Captain Ryman and his men came ashore in Nashville to look in on a revival meeting that Jones was holding in a tent at Broad and Spruce streets. Their customary practice on such outings was to harass the revivalist and break up the meeting. Records differ about the subject of Jones's sermon that day; some say that his topic was "Mother"; some say "Whiskey." Accounts agree, however, that it was a rousing sermon. It made an immediate and devoted follower of Tom Ryman, who promptly closed the bars on all his steamers, confiscated the liquor, converted his big dockside saloon to a religious meeting hall, and began a vigorous campaign to build an auditorium for Jones to preach in. Ryman gave generously of his own money for the proposed tabernacle and worked tirelessly to raise funds from other sources. In 1888, Sam Jones again came to Nashville to hold a revival, and $22,000 contributed at his final sermon went into the Tabernacle Fund.

The hand-cut limestone foundation was laid that summer. On February 25, 1889, a charter of incorporation registered with the State of Tennessee gave the Union Gospel Tabernacle as the name of the proposed building and the promotion of religion and morality as its purpose.

On March 25, 1890, with the walls of the unfinished Tabernacle six feet high and canvas stretched across the top for a roof, the Reverend Sam Jones held the auditorium's first meeting. For the next decade, Jones helped raise money to pay off the debt on the building which his zeal had inspired. Architect A. T. Thompson, who designed the Tabernacle, and a number of the men who helped build it worked for less than their usual rates as a contribution to the enterprise. The people of Nashville continued to

1. Ellen Beasley "The End of the Rainbow," *Historic Preservation*, p. 21.

Ryman Auditorium
Nashville

give money for it at revival meetings and through various organizations. In 1900, it was announced that a single individual, Captain Tom Ryman, had carried forward the building debt and the interest on it.[2]

Though original plans had included a balcony which would enable the building to seat 6,000, the new Tabernacle consisted at first of a ground floor only, accommodating approximately half that number. Curved wooden pews surrounded a pulpit and a small platform. There was no stage.

Preparing for the Tennessee Centennial Celebration in Nashville in 1897, many state organizations planned annual conventions in the capital to coincide with the celebration. When the biggest group of all, the Confederate Veterans Association, announced that it would convene at the Tabernacle and that 60,000 to 100,000 members would probably attend, it became clear that the building would need full seating capacity. The veterans' convention was scheduled for June 1897; the new balcony, anchored on steel columns extending to the basement, was completed in late May, and the Union Gospel Tabernacle became the South's largest assembly hall.[3] After the convention, the Confederate Veterans Association donated money to pay for the balcony, known since then as the Confederate Gallery.

Since public funds went into the building's construction, Nashvillians felt that the Tabernacle might be put to public use as needed, and it early began serving as an assembly hall for conventions, lectures, fund-raising campaigns, political speeches, recitals, and musical programs. Memorial services for well-known public figures, local and national, were also held there. One of the most significant in the building's history occurred on December 25, 1904, when the Reverend Sam Jones conducted Captain Tom Ryman's funeral. More than 4,000 people were present. At the end of the service, when Jones proposed that the name of the building be changed to the Ryman Auditorium, the proposal was unanimously approved.[4]

The Ryman's stage was built in 1901, when a fund-raising committee, co-operating with the Nashville Philharmonic Society, helped to bring the Metropolitan Opera to Nashville—and a stage became a necessity. Completed, the stage was so big that it permitted the company to present *The Barber of Seville* on "the most elaborate scale."[5] It also reduced the building's seating capacity to 3,500, but it gave Nashville an auditorium which could accommodate other opera companies, concert performers, and theater groups.

Further work was done on the stage in 1904, when the French Grand Opera Company of New Orleans came, and it was modified to provide dressing rooms and property storage in 1906, when Sarah Bernhardt appeared in *Camille*.[6]

Within the next few decades, Nashville audiences at the Ryman had heard the Chicago, the Boston, and the New York Symphony orchestras, as well as Sousa's band and the U. S. Marine Band. Victor Herbert conducted his orchestra for the May Music Festival of 1903.

With the popularity of lyceums and chautauquas in 1904, the auditorium's trustees contracted with the Rice Lyceum Bureau for a year's series of lectures, music, readings, and entertainment. Paderewski appeared in 1907, as did William Jennings Bryan, Carrie Nation, and Emma Calvé. Audiences at the Ryman heard lectures by Russell H. Conwell and Booker T. Washington, and Louise Homer, leading contralto of the Metropolitan Opera, appeared in concert. Helen Keller and her teacher Anne Sullivan Macy appeared in 1913, and Pavlova, Tetrazzini, and Alma Gluck came the following year. Galli-Curci sang in 1918; and in 1919,

2. Jerry Henderson, "Nashville's Ryman Auditorium," p. 308.
3. *Ibid.*, p. 317.

4. Beasley, "The End of the Rainbow," p. 21.
5. Nashville *American*, October 23, 1901.
6. Beasley, "The End of the Rainbow," p. 21; Henderson, "Nashville's Ryman Auditorium," p. 326.

Gospel tabernacle pews look down on a modern world of electronic gear.

Ryman Auditorium
Nashville

Paul Ryman, tenor, appeared in recital in the auditorium named for his father. Enrico Caruso sang there, the same year. Mischa Elman played the Ryman in 1920. Billy Sunday, Maurice Evans, Helen Hayes, Katherine Cornell, Maude Adams, Otis Skinner, Marian Anderson, Arthur Rubinstein, Bob Hope, Doris Day, and many other famous people have appeared there. Tex Ritter, Roy Acuff, Hank Williams, and Eddy Arnold centered their careers there.

The auditorium attained national prominence in the 1920s, when Nashville's last legitimate theater was converted to a vaudeville and motion picture house, and the Ryman became the only place in the city where legitimate theater, concerts, and recitals could be held.[7]

Beginning in 1941, the Ryman became the home of WSM's Grand Ole Opry, after the country music show, established in 1925, had progressively outgrown rented quarters in studio after studio, and its crowds justified the move into "the largest house in Middle Tennessee."[8]

Physical changes to the Ryman have been minor, and structural changes virtually unnecessary. The Gothic-revival structure has remained much the same as when it was built. The original pews and wooden floors remain. Lancet windows are spaced along the brick walls, and a buttressed effect appears at the corners and down the sides. The Louisville Bridge and Iron Company built the truss roof, which was outlined with trefoils on the stepped gables.[9] In 1957, the building was sandblasted and cleaned, the wooden doors were replaced with aluminum and glass ones, and a new dressing room was built.

Some improvements have been made since National Life and Accident Insurance Company bought the auditorium. A new gas furnace was installed, and offices were added alongside the stage. For the taping of the Johnny Cash Show on television, the stage itself was modified. A removable stage and special lighting were added.

The future of the old auditorium is uncertain. The present owners plan to move the Grand Ole Opry to a new auditorium now under construction in Opryland, the company's amusement-entertainment park along the Cumberland River. Announced plans were to raze the old Ryman and, as a sentimental salute to its eighty-odd years as a colorful part of Nashville's cultural life, use part of the materials salvaged from it to build a Little Church of Opryland. Since a number of people and organizations, including the National Trust for Historic Preservation, would like to see the Ryman preserved, however, National Life and Accident Insurance Company decided to leave the decision about the Ryman's future until a later time.

BIBLIOGRAPHY

Beasley, Ellen. "The End of the Rainbow." *Historic Preservation*, 24, No. 1 (January-March 1972), 19–23.
Henderson, Jerry. "Nashville's Ryman Auditorium." *Tennessee Historical Quarterly*, XXVII (Winter 1968), 305–328.
Nashville, Tennessee. WSM Broadcasting Company. "History of the Grand Ole Opry House."

7. Beasley, "The End of the Rainbow," p. 21.
8. *Ibid.*
9. *Ibid.*

To Opry audiences, the textures of timeworn wood, metal, and stone are part of the performance.

Ryman Auditorium
Nashville

The huge size of the barnlike Ryman echoes the earlier tradition of cavernous tobacco warehouses.

Union Station

NASHVILLE'S Union Station, at 1001 Broadway, is one of the city's unique and inspired architectural landmarks. The handsome gray stone building, with its gables and domes and towers, is one of the country's last surviving grand turn-of-the-century railroad stations. Built co-operatively by the Louisville and Nashville Railroad and the Nashville, Chattanooga, and St. Louis Railway, its monumental opulence symbolized the power and prestige of the railroads in the latter part of the nineteenth century.

Ground was broken for the railroad terminal and office building on August 1, 1898, after the razing of some 200 various buildings and the removal of 220,000 cubic yards of earth and rock from the site. The building was formally opened on October 9, 1900.

Union Station was designed in the Richardsonian Romanesque Revival style by Richard Montfort, first Chief Engineer of the Louisville and Nashville Railroad and later Chief Engineer of the Louisville and Nashville Terminal Company which was formed to administer the project. The courthouse of Allegheny County, Pennsylvania (1884–1886), designed by H. H. Richardson, one of the most admired architects of the period, was Montfort's inspiration for the design.

The slate-roofed, 150-foot-square building is constructed of Bowling Green gray stone and Tennessee marble. It contains three stories and an attic and is flanked by the baggage, mail, and express building and, at the rear, by the enormous iron and steel train shed—noteworthy engineering achievements in themselves.

The square central tower on the front façade is 220 feet tall. For half a century, it stood 239 feet tall,[1] the extra height being provided at its top by a bronze statue of Mercury which had originally decorated the Commerce Building at the Tennessee Centennial Exposition in 1897. On March 24, 1952, buffeted by high winds, the huge statue fell to the tracks below.

The statue was never restored to its former place atop the tower because of the certain expense and the possible hazards that that would have occasioned. A second, shorter, arcaded tower, topped with flying buttresses supporting a huge enclosed chimney which is still in use, appears at the rear of the terminal building.[2]

The train shed to the rear, built, according to a contemporary account,[3] partly by Terminal Company workmen and partly by the Louisville Bridge and Iron Company, measures 250 feet by 500 feet, with a clear span of 200 feet. All parts of the truss except the rafters are of steel beams and rods. Its original slate roof extended over tracks that could accommodate ten full-length trains.

The central terminal building was constructed at a cost of $350,000. The train shed cost $200,000, and the freight terminal, $100,000.[4]

The central waiting room inside is a three-story light-well measuring 67 feet by 125 feet. Its dome is 63 feet tall, with a barrel-vaulted skylight originally bearing "art glass" in art nouveau colors and designs. Wall and ceiling finish are of Tennessee marble and painted plaster with wooden wainscotting. The main floor is ceramic tile. Until recently a restaurant, shops, ticket and baggage counter surrounded the open central area. At the rear is a large stone fireplace no longer used. The building was originally heated by chambered boilers from which hot air was conveyed to a 5-foot-deep area 150 feet square, directly beneath the floor of the central waiting room.[5] This system is no longer used; heat is now provided electrically.

Two wooden stairways, one on either side of the central waiting room, lead upward to the mezzanine and the second and third floors. A third stairway begins at the second-floor level

1. Thomas B. Brumbaugh, "The Architecture of Nashville's Union Station," p. 5.

2. *Ibid.*, p. 6.
3. Nashville *American*, October 9, 1900.
4. Brumbaugh, "The Architecture of Nashville's Union Station," p. 6.
5. Nashville *American*, October 9, 1900.

Rusticated textures of stone stand in bold contrast to a growing city of steel and glass.

50 in the front of the building and extends to the full height of the front tower.

Interconnecting offices on the second floor are entered from a balcony on sculptured brackets cantilevered over and on the full perimeter of the waiting room, with wrought-iron railings and wooden top rail. Original brass and wrought-iron railings are still in use in the building, both inside and out.

Several "safe" rooms, with steel combination doors, are located on various floors.

Special decorative features of the interior are the scenes sculptured in bas relief in the plaster over the second-floor balcony and the clocks at the north and south ends of the waiting room. The art work was done by M. J. Donner, a Chicago sculptor. On the station's formal opening day, the Nashville *American* described the interior:

This is altogether the most magnificent and artistic—in color, configuration, and furnishing—first floor of any station in America.

As one enters the new station . . . the first attraction is the loggia, a massive lot of arches and entablature . . . elaborately carved in stone, panelled in oak, and paved with granite and tiling.

Passing through the vestibules, by means of the three heavy stone archways, all beautifully carved in the Romanesque, one is first impressed with the color scheme of the general waiting room. . . . No color-blind people touched this work. Not a false tint has been imparted. . . . The lower section . . . is dark colonial green, touched with darker green and gold, and capped with a cornice of gold. The next is two shades lighter green, with corners of yellow or mauve, the high lights being brought out in gold. [Upward] the green still lightens, till it goes out in yellow and green configurations in the dome panels that blend with the wonderful color and design of the art glass in the skylights above.[6]

Five stucco arches appear on each side of the central waiting room—the east and west walls. Female figures of heroic size are executed in bas relief on either side of each arch, each figure presenting a product carried by the railroads. Facing each other across the length of the room,

the north and south end walls show, respectively, painted bas relief representations of a train—"the 1900 limited—a full vestibuled passenger train, with the Nashville and Chattanooga bully engine No. 108 at the head"[7] and the Egyptian pharoah Rameses the Great with his queen, riding in a chariot drawn by slaves.

With the exception of Mercury's absence from the pinnacle of the front tower, Union Station today is little changed from its original appearance. Escalators were installed in 1948.[8] The end truss of the train shed as it joins the gallery at the rear of the main terminal building has been modified to accommodate installation of modern loading equipment. Other differences are the repairing or replacement of original equipment or furnishings with substitutes less spectacular than the originals. Much of the colorful charm of the once splendid interior is overlaid by accumulated layers of grime.

6. *Ibid.*

7. *Ibid.*
8. Brumbaugh, "The Architecture of Nashville's Union Station," p. 6.

Union Station
Nashville

BIBLIOGRAPHY

Brumbaugh, Thomas B. "The Architecture of Nashville's Union Station." *Tennessee Historical Quarterly*, XXVII (Spring 1968), 3–12.

Burt, Jesse C. "Four Decades of the Nashville, Chattanooga and St. Louis Railroad, 1873–1916." *Tennessee Historical Quarterly*, X (December 1951), 320–333.

Burt, Jesse C. *Nashville. Its Life and Times*. Nashville: Tennessee Book Company, 1959.

Creighton, Wilbur F. *Building of Nashville*. Nashville: Wilbur F. Creighton, Jr., 1969.

Franklin, Corinne. "Union Station Holds to Prideful Heritage." Nashville *Banner*, September 25, 1964.

Herndon, Marion. "Union Station: Silent Sentinel."

Nashville *Tennessean Magazine*, January 5, 1964, pp. 29–30.

Nashville *American*, January 23, 1897.

Nashville *American*, August 1, 1898.

Nashville *American*, October 9, 1900.

Prince, Richard E. *Nashville, Chattanooga & St. Louis Railway. History and Steam Locomotives*. Green River, Wyoming: Richard E. Prince, 1967.

Tennessee. Davidson County. Chancery Court.

Tennessee. Davidson County. Register's Office.

Waller, William, editor. *Nashville in the 1890s*. Nashville: Vanderbilt University Press, 1970.

Wooldridge, John, editor. *History of Nashville, Tennessee*. Nashville: H. W. Crew, 1890.

Shadows through the intricate tracery of wrought iron were a greeting to late-afternoon travelers.

Union Station
Nashville

Ornament and function both create abstract effects.

The Public Arcade

ALTHOUGH Lebanon, Tennessee, boasts a small arcade, Nashville's Public Arcade, between Fourth and Fifth avenues, North, is the one major use of this type of building in the Middle Tennessee area. Early nineteenth-century experiments with cast-iron and glass structures led to the erection of many such buildings at home and abroad.

As country towns became cities, and downtown property increased tremendously in value during the nineteenth century, private alleys were seen to be adaptable for commercial use. It is only remarkable that Nashville was to wait until 1902 to take advantage of Overton Alley and build its first "shopping center" there, in the form of the Public Arcade. The alley it occupies was originally named for John Overton, Andrew Jackson's law partner, and the area is still occasionally called by that name.

The prime mover in the erection of the Public Arcade was David C. Buntin, prominent Nashville realtor and banker. At least two members of the Buntin family, among others, held rights to the alley property and they persuaded owners of other property facing Fourth and Fifth avenues that an arcade would be a lucrative and attractive development. With Hugh L. Craighead, Charles Buntin, T. M. Steger, and J. Lee Bland, Buntin formed a corporation which was chartered under the laws of Tennessee in 1901, and construction was begun. The pioneer shopping mall opened in 1902.

Walter Stokes, Jr., president of the Arcade Company, Inc., for the past thirty-three years, thinks that David Buntin, while on a trip abroad, was impressed by the famous Galleria Vittorio Emmanuele (1865–77) in Milan. Buntin may also have known the Cleveland, Ohio, Arcade of 1890, which is the largest American example.

In Nashville's Arcade, identical Palladian façades mark the entrances on Fourth and Fifth avenues, but otherwise the building has no exterior aspect, since it is surrounded on its long sides by other structures. The Arcade is two stories tall, with shops and offices on two levels, the second level featuring galleries on all four sides, protected by cast-iron balustrades. It is open to pedestrian traffic only. The original four stairways leading to the upper level have now been reduced to three; there is also a small elevator.

The Edgefield and Nashville Manufacturing Company designed the structure. It is not known whether any specific architect drew up the plans. The rolled steel bracing system used to support the pitched roof of wire-reinforced plate glass was fabricated by the Nashville Bridge Company. Originally 360 feet long, 84 feet wide, and 56 feet high, the structure has been modified somewhat by later renovations.

Although it was never innovative in any way and appeared late in the development of such buildings, the Public Arcade is attractive and relatively spacious. The Cleveland Arcade is only thirty feet longer, though it is nearly three times greater in height and thus more gracefully proportioned. Nashville's Arcade was placed on the National Register of Historic Places in February 1973.

A typical late-nineteenth-century urban form, the arcade expressed a strong sense of communal life.

St. Mary's Cathedral
(St. Mary's Church, Roman Catholic)

ST. MARY'S Cathedral at 328 Fifth Avenue, North, in Nashville, was designed by William Strickland, the well-known architect who also designed the Tennessee State Capitol and Nashville's First Presbyterian Church.

St. Mary's is a simple, well-proportioned Greek revival building with excellent details, and Strickland is said to have considered it his best ecclesiastical design. Construction began in 1844 and the cathedral was dedicated on October 31, 1847. The crypt of Bishop Richard P. Miles, the man largely responsible for the cathedral's being built, lies beneath its great altar. Father Abram Ryan, the "Poet Priest of the South," served as assistant pastor from 1864 to 1865.

In 1914, the New Cathedral of the Incarnation was built on West End Avenue, and St. Mary's Cathedral became a parish church.

The building faces west on Fifth Avenue, North, adjacent to the State Capitol. South of the church, connected to it by a corridor on the main level, is the rectory. The chancery office building is directly behind the church, across an alley.

The exterior walls were originally of brick—whether stuccoed or painted is not clear from available records. Today, the walls are of gray pressed brick, with a gray stone facing on the front, or west façade. For many years, this stone façade was thought to have been part of the original structure. Documents recently discovered, however, in the vault of the Nashville chancery office, provide conclusive evidence that the exterior walls of the original building were entirely of brick. These documents included plans and specifications prepared in 1926 for alterations to the church building by the Nashville architectural firm of Asmus and Clark, and stated that the "walls of the entrance porch . . . shall be veneered with face brick . . . laid directly against the existing brick."[1] An addendum to these specifications then states that the façade, or "West Elevation," instead of being veneered with face brick, as first specified, was to be "veneered with Nashville Travatine [sic] Stone,"[2] a trade name for a local grade of dense limestone.

The remodeling of that year—the first major alteration for which there are available descriptive records—included the setting of two fluted Ionic stone columns into the half portico, replacing the original columns, thought to have been brick or stucco. New stone bases were provided, but the original stone capitals were cleaned and reset. The frieze and parapet of the main cornice and the pediment panel over the portico were restuccoed. Existing windows and frames in the nave were replaced with new double-hung windows glazed with cathedral glass. Quartered white-oak doors were installed in the three entrance doorways off the front portico. Iron gates were installed in the front portico, set within the openings among the two columns and corner pilasters.

The original belfry, over the west end of the building, was also modified in 1926. Its wood framing was repaired and new sashes and panes were installed in the four cruciform windows. Two procedures, however, did much to alter its earlier effect of balance and proportion: the circular arcade on the top story was, for the first time, closed off with metal louvers, and the circular clock faces that alternated with the cruciform windows in the bays below were removed, and the bays were left without any opening or surface articulation.

No evidence has been found to indicate what the original appearance of the interior might have been. An account written in 1870 describes it:

There is one main entrance on the west side, leading up from a flight of stone steps . . . A triple archway divides a spacious vestibule from the auditorium. In the center of this archway stands the holy font. The

---

1. Asmus and Clark, Architects, "Alterations to Saint Mary's Church, Fifth Avenue, & Cedar Street, Nashville, Tennessee."

2. Asmus and Clark, Architects, "Addenda to Specifications, St. Mary's Church, Nashville, Tennessee."

St. Mary's Cathedral, Roman Catholic
Nashville

inside of the auditorium is well-arranged, and has three aisles separating six rows of pews . . . capable of seating from 900 to 1,000 persons. The chancel is divided from the auditorium by a small balustrade stretching full length across the house. In the gallery . . . which extends across the building at the western extremity, is a splendid organ . . . bought in 1849 . . . encased in oak, and . . . of Grecian architecture.[3]

In 1947, in connection with the centennial anniversary of the cathedral's dedication, the basement was remodeled into the Bishop Miles Chapel, to perpetuate the memory of the man who played such a large part in the church's founding.

A new organ, using the pipes of the old one, was installed as part of the centennial project, and the building's exterior and interior were refurbished.

BIBLIOGRAPHY

Asmus & Clark, Architects. *Alterations to Saint Mary's Church, Fifth Ave., & Cedar St., Nashville, Tennessee.* Working Drawings, Commission No. 596. Nashville: Office of Amus & Clark, 1926.

Asmus & Clark, Architects. *Specifications for Remodeling & Additions for St. Mary's Church: Fifth Ave., & Cedar St., Nashville, Tennessee.* Commission No. 596. Nashville: Office of Asmus & Clark, 1926.

Asmus & Clark, Architects. *Addenda to Specifications. St. Mary's Church, Nashville, Tennessee.* Nashville: Office of Asmus & Clark, 1926.

Barr, Daniel F. *Souvenir of St. Mary's Cathedral, Including the Century's Annals of the Roman Catholic Church in Nashville.* Nashville: Burton & Fick, 1897.

The Catholic Advocate, November 20, 1847.

Cochran, Gifford A. *Grandeur in Tennessee. Classical Revival Architecture in a Pioneer State.* New York: J. J. Augustin, 1946.

Federal Writers' Project. *Tennessee: A Guide to the State.* New York: Viking Press, 1939.

3. Charles E. Roberts, *Nashville and Her Trade for 1870,* pp. 453–454.

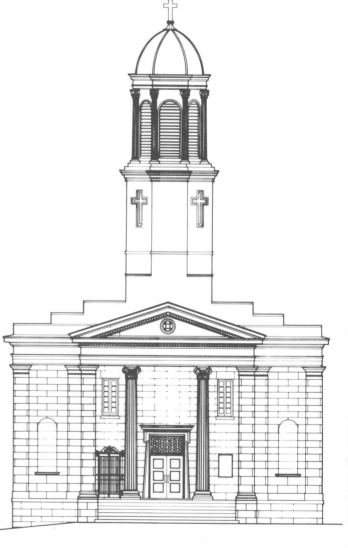

Southwest Elevation
HABS drawings by Donna Gay Woodrum and Robert J. Dunay, 1970
Traced from drawings by Asmus & Clark, Architects, July 14, 1926

61

Gilchrist, Agnes A. *William Strickland, Architect and Engineer, 1788–1854.* Philadelphia: University of Pennsylvania Press, 1950.

Nashville *Banner*, January 19, 1930.

Nashville *Banner*, July 30, 1967.

Nashville *Daily Union*, November 3, 1847.

O'Daniel, V. F. *The Father of the Church in Tennessee, or the Life, Times, and Character of the Right Reverend Richard Pius Miles, O.P., the First Bishop of Nashville.* Washington, D.C.: The Cominicana, 1926.

Old St. Mary's. An Historical Sketch of St. Mary's Church, Nashville, Tennessee, 1847–1947. Nashville: Cullum & Ghertner Co., 1947.

Republican Banner, November 5, 1847.

Southern Engineering & Appraisal Company. *Appraisal: Saint Mary's Church and Saint Mary's Rectory, Fifth Ave., & Cedar St.* Nashville: Office of the Southern Engineering & Appraisal Co., 1933.

Tennessee. Davidson County. County Court Clerk's Office.

Tennessee. Davidson County. Register's Office.

Wooldridge, John, editor. *History of Nashville, Tennessee.* Nashville: H. W. Crew, 1890.

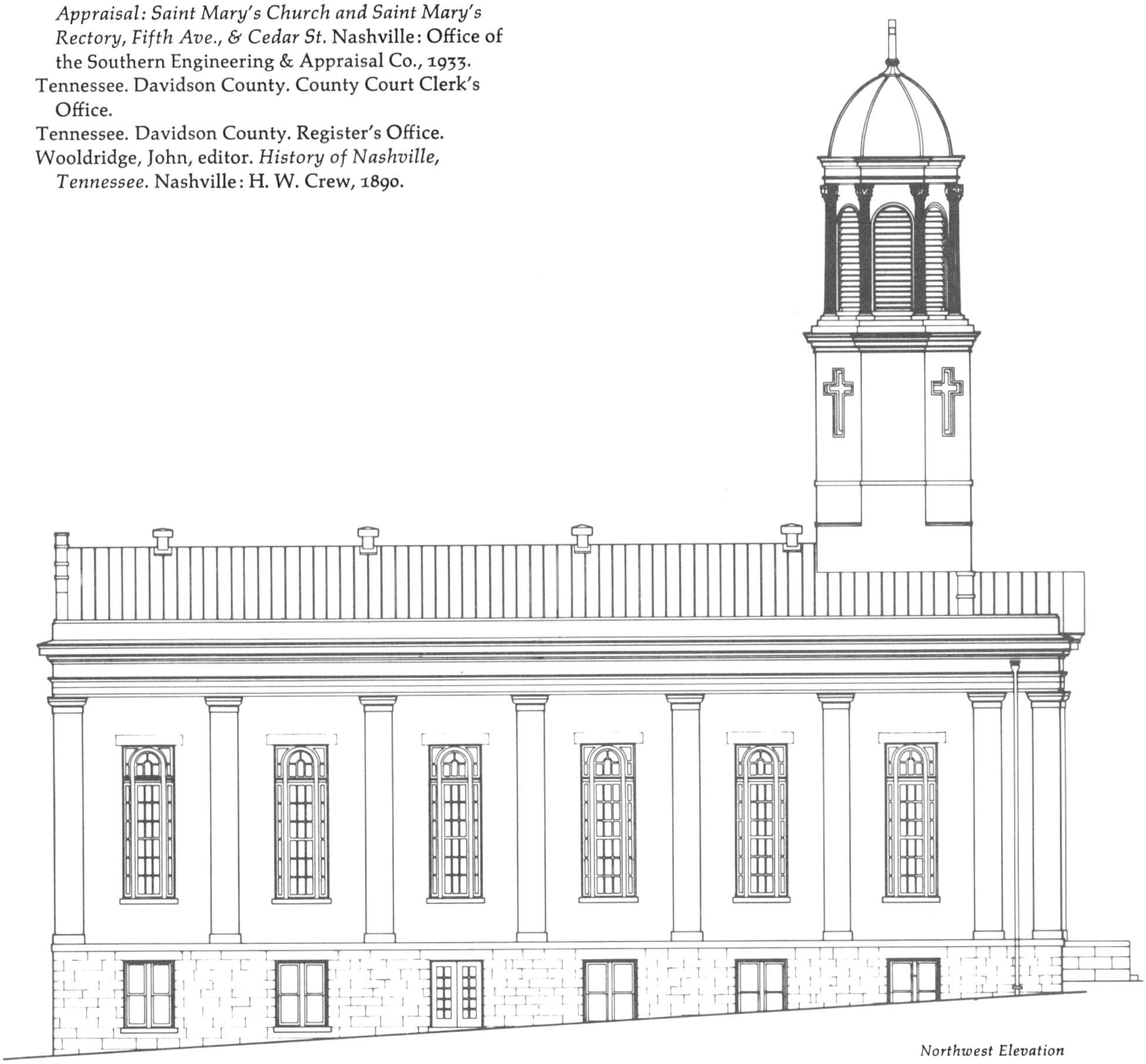

Northwest Elevation

St. Mary's Cathedral, Roman Catholic
Nashville

St. Mary's embodies another interpretation of classic design for a Roman Catholic church.

First Presbyterian Church

(*Downtown Presbyterian Church*)

WHAT is now Nashville's Downtown Presbyterian Church, at the corner of Fifth Avenue and Church Street (154 Fifth Avenue, North), was, from 1849 to 1955, the First Presbyterian Church. The name was changed in 1955, when the First Presbyterian Church relocated at Oak Hill and Franklin Road. Some members of the congregation who wanted to maintain the old building and the work of the church there purchased the property at Fifth and Church and organized the Downtown Presbyterian Church.

The building, designed by William Strickland—who also designed the Tennessee State Capitol and St. Mary's Cathedral in Nashville—is the largest, best-preserved example of an Egyptian-revival church building in America.

Today's Downtown Presbyterian Church building is the third to occupy the Fifth Avenue site, a parcel of land conveyed by Randal McGavock to the trustees of the Nashville Presbyterian Church whose membership, formally organized in 1814, became known as the First Presbyterian Church. In the first church built on the site, in 1816, Andrew Jackson was presented a sword by the State of Tennessee for his services at the Battle of New Orleans. This church, which burned in 1832, was replaced by a second building, which also burned, in 1848, and the present one was begun by Strickland the following year. The cornerstone was laid on April 28, 1849, and the church was dedicated on Easter Sunday, April 20, 1851.

Facing north toward Church Street, the rectangular building measures 75 feet 4 inches by 135 feet 5 inches. Walls of natural-finish brick top foundations of Tennessee limestone. The portico on the north entrance has two Egyptian columns with a sheet-metal entablature. There are two towers, one on either side of the north portico, with cornices of corbeled brick. The doors at the main entry have four recessed panels, the two at top and bottom nearly square, with two rectangular vertical panels between. Seven brick chimneys rise above the simple pitched roof. The triple-hung windows are of stained glass.

The interior of the building was originally different from its appearance today: the auditorium was larger, because the rooms at either side of the pulpit did not exist, the spaces being used as "amen corners"; the windows were of clear glass and had inside shutters; the balcony originally came farther out and down into the nave and was supported by columns; finally, the walls were gray, and the ceiling was smooth, with none of the brilliant colors that are there now.

The first alterations and remodeling occurred after Federal forces had occupied the church building from January to August of 1863 and again from October 1863 to 1865. The building was used as a hospital, beds for the wounded filling the auditorium. Horses, stabled in what is now the church's dining room, left hoof prints that are still visible in the flooring beneath the linoleum. The church was restored to something like its original appearance with $7,500 received for damages from Federal authorities.[1]

In 1867, the church bell was given by Adelicia Acklen. The bell was made in West Troy, New York, weighed 4,000 pounds, and cost $3,000. For many years, it was used as the city fire alarm.

In 1880, two columns were added to the west façade.

Extensive alterations were made in 1881, however, and it was then that the interior was given its present appearance. The balcony was reduced in size. The "amen corners" were enclosed to create separate rooms. The frescoed perspective above the doors to these rooms, showing Egyptian columns receding into the distance, as well as the perspective painting on the altar wall, were also added at this time. The ceiling was coffered, with rosettes at beam intersections, and the square recessed panels were rendered with bits of blue sky and clouds. The existing curved walnut pews were installed to replace the earlier box pews with

1. Jesse E. Wills, "An Echo from Egypt: A History of the Building Occupied by the First Presbyterian Church, Nashville, Tennessee," p. 70.

66 doors, and new gas chandeliers (since replaced) also were installed.

The symbolic colors and decorations, derived from the symbolism of Egyptian temples, were added during this remodeling. The color red represents divine love; blue, divine intelligence; golden yellow, the mercy of God. The lilies are symbolic of innocence and purity; the triangle, the Trinity. The cluster of seeds held together with a band of gold crossed with red represents the membership held together with a gold band of love. The winged globe signifies eternity; the serpent, wisdom; the wings, the soul.

In 1887, the final change was made to bring the interior to its present appearance. The inside shutters were removed and the present stained-glass windows were installed. In this same year, steam heat was installed.

In 1898, the interior was repainted, without altering the decor. A Frenchman named De LaMotte did the work.

Other special decorative features of the interior today are the solid black-walnut altar and trim surrounding the organ pipes. The present organ was installed in 1913, requiring some changes in the choir loft behind the pulpit platform.

A new Sunday School building, designed by Nashville architect Henry Hibbs, was begun to the rear of the church during World War I and was completed in 1919.

In 1937, extensive structural work costing $37,893.41 was done, and the interior was renovated again, but without altering the design.

BIBLIOGRAPHY

Bunting, Robert F. *Manual of the Presbyterian Church, Nashville, Tennessee, with a Brief History from its Organization, November 1814, to November 1868.* Nashville: Southern Methodist Publishing House, 1868.

W. W. Clayton. "First Presbyterian Church of Nashville." In *History of Davidson County, Tennessee, with Illustrations and Biographical Sketches of its Prominent Men*, pp. 312–313. Philadelphia: J. W. Lewis & Co., 1880.

Cochran, Gifford A. *Grandeur in Tennessee*. New York: J. J. Augustin, 1946.

"The Downtown Presbyterian Church. A Brief History." N.p.d. Brief historical vignette available at the Downtown Presbyterian Church, Nashville.

Federal Writers' Project. *Tennessee: A Guide to the State*. New York: Viking Press, 1939.

The First Presbyterian Church. One Hundred Years of Service. Addresses Delivered in Connection with the Observance of the One Hundredth Anniversary, November 8–15, 1914. Nashville: Foster & Parkes, 1915.

Gilchrist, Agnes A. *William Strickland. Architect and Engineer, 1788–1854*, pp. 17, 114–115. Philadelphia: University of Philadelphia Press, 1950.

Nashville, Tennessee. Tennessee State Library and Archives. Records, First Presbyterian Church.

Roberts, Charles E. "First Presbyterian Church." In *Nashville and Her Trade for 1870*, pp. 437–440. Nashville: Roberts & Purvis, 1870.

Tennessee. Davidson County. Register's Office.

Wills, Jesse E. "An Echo from Egypt. A History of the Building Occupied by the First Presbyterian Church, Nashville, Tennessee." *Tennessee Historical Quarterly*, XI (March 1952), 63–77.

Wills, Jesse E. "The Towers See One Hundred Years. The Story of the First Presbyterian Church Building, Nashville, Tennessee." Pamphlet. April 12, 1951.

Wooldridge, John, editor. *History of Nashville, Tennessee*. Nashville: H. W. Crew, 1890.

Zion Presbyterian Church

AN interesting example of rural church architecture in the South is Zion Presbyterian Church in Maury County, 1 mile south of Highway 99, 6.3 miles west of Columbia. It has been in continuous use since its completion in 1849.

The severe architectural style of the building reflects the stern tenets of the Presbyterians who built it. Its decoration is limited to such structural adornments as the stepped gables and recessed open vestibule, both of which are frequently found on houses of the period in Middle Tennessee. The structure has been changed very little since it was built. It is 80 feet long by 50 feet broad, with walls of natural brick on foundations of Tennessee limestone. Corbeling appears on the solid masonry walls, and the north and south walls have stepped parapets. There is a recessed porch on the south side.

Zion Presbyterian Church stands on part of an eight-square-mile tract of land purchased for $15,360 in 1807 by a colony of eleven Presbyterian families. It is the third Presbyterian church to occupy the site. The first, a log building erected in 1807, was supplanted by a brick structure in 1813.

A three-man committee composed of the Reverend James M. Arnell, Samuel H. Armstrong, and John D. Fleming submitted two plans for Zion Presbyterian Church when it was decided to build in 1846. The plans were substantially the same, but the one chosen allowed for a gallery above an open vestibule, for the accommodation of black people in the congregation.[1]

The new church was occupied for the first time on Saturday, April 7, 1849. The first sermon was preached by the Reverend N. A. Penlam of Tuscumbia, Alabama.

In 1906, an iron fence was built around the churchyard, the money for it having been left in the will of Mrs. Edward Armstrong. The church windows are stained glass now, but there is a question as to when they were installed. Robert Livingston Armstrong, a trustee of the church, believes that they were installed when the church was built, but indicates that they might date from an 1887 remodeling.

The church's first pastor was Dr. James White Stephenson, who was also the instructor at the academy which stood near the church. It was said of Dr. Stephenson that he trained his charges in honesty, integrity, and the Golden Rule, along with their academic work. One of his students was the future president of the United States, James K. Polk, who enrolled for classes at the age of seventeen.

BIBILIOGRAPHY

Armstrong, Robert Livingston. "Places of Historical Interest." Unpublished manuscript. Highway 99, Cross Bridges, Tennessee, Zion Community.

Fleming, W. S. *Historical Sketch of Zion Church, Maury County, Tennessee, and the Genealogy of the Frierson Family*. Columbia, Tennessee: Aydelott's Printery, 1907.

Highsaw, Mary Wagner. "A History of Zion Community in Maury County, 1806–60." *Tennessee Historical Quarterly*, V (March 1946), 18–22.

---

1. W. S. Fleming, *Historical Sketch of Zion Church, Maury County, Tennessee, and the Genealogy of the Frierson Family*, p. 25.

Old Presbyterian values show themselves in disciplined architectural forms.

Zion Presbyterian Church
Columbia

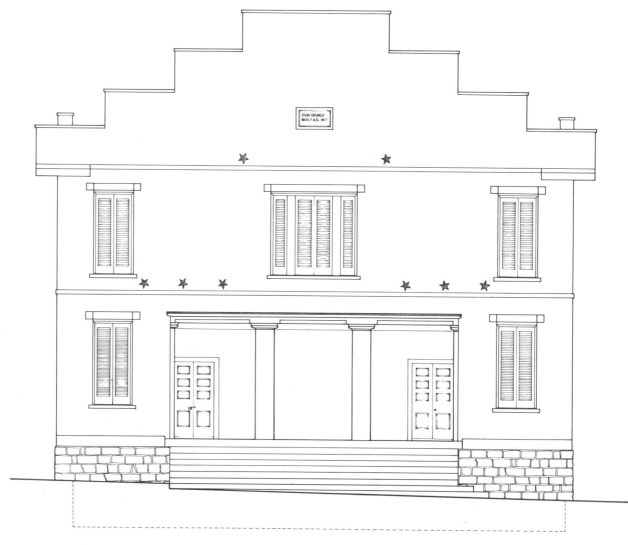

Front Elevation
HABS drawing by Gilbert M. Glaubinger, 1971

Holy Trinity Episcopal Church

HOLY TRINITY Episcopal Church, at 615 Sixth Avenue, South, in Nashville, is one of the outstanding examples of the early Gothic revival style in Tennessee. It was modeled after an English parish church.

The design for it is attributed to the architectural firm of Wills and Dudley of New York; it reflects a type of design for which Frank Wills of that firm was renowned.

The building occupies a site given by M. W. Wetmore in 1850. It has remained the property of the parish of the Church of the Holy Trinity since its construction—completion of which took place over a period of several years. The cornerstone was laid in 1852, and the chancel was completed in 1853, but the tower was not completed until 1887. It appeared then much as it is today.

A contemporary account says that the church

is . . . built of [native] blue limestone, and with its open [hammer beam] roof of varnished cedar and its deep recessed chancel it is, indeed, a pure and beautiful piece of architecture. Its altar is of cedar, and a crown of thorns adorns the center of its frontal. The nave is 70 by 25 feet, and has a seating capacity of 250 people.[1]

The original roofing was seamed tin, replaced at an unknown date by asbestos cement shingles. The present roofing is composition material.

Photographs made in 1940 show the battlements that originally crowned the turret, but they have since been removed, having become dislodged and considered unsafe.

In 1862, the church building was taken over by the Federal army for use as a powder magazine and a place to quarter horses. The interior and furnishings underwent considerable damage. A late-nineteenth-century writer recorded that the troopers smashed the stained-glass window in the chancel, used the altar to cut meat on, used the font as a wash basin, and carried away the organ, piece by

1. W. W. Clayton, *History of Davidson County, Tennessee*, pp. 337–338.

North Elevation
HABS drawing by Donna Gay Woodrum, 1970

Nostalgia for the English parish church was an important factor for nineteenth-century Episcopalians.

74 piece.[2] Subsequently, the U.S. government proposed to pay damages, and eventually did pay $1,333 for this purpose.

Holy Trinity Episcopal Church was first used by Negro worshipers in 1895. The present Negro congregation was organized in 1902 and was officially made a mission of the Episcopal Church for Negroes in 1907.

It is difficult to determine all the alterations since the church was built, but records for some exist.

Between 1866 and 1867, in part through Christ Church and the Church of the Advent, a carpet for the chancel, matting for the aisle, and an organ were bought. The chancel window was restored at this time.

In 1868, a small frame room was erected on the church lot for a school.

A new pipe organ was purchased in 1872 by a Mr. Fisher.

The vestry room was enlarged in 1883.

In 1893, a new set of seats was obtained.

In 1952, new doors were hung, floors and pews were repaired, and the interior generally redecorated. Lawn lights were installed.

The present pulpit is not original, but was brought from New York about 1935. Much of the stained glass is also not original.

In 1964, air-conditioning was installed.

BIBLIOGRAPHY

Beard, William E. "The Church of Ante-Bellum Times." In *Christ Church, Nashville, 1829–1929*, pp. 73–89. Anne Rankin, editor in chief. Nashville: Marshall & Bruce, 1929.

Clayton, W. W. "Church of the Holy Trinity." In *History of Davidson County, Tennessee, with Illustrations and Biographical Sketches of Its Prominent Men*, by W. W. Clayton, pp. 337–338. Philadelphia: J. W. Lewis & Co., 1880.

Federal Writers' Project. *Tennessee: A Guide to the State*. New York: Viking Press, 1939.

Green, William M. *Memoir of Rt. Rev. James Hervey Otey, D.D., LL.D., the First Bishop of Tennessee.* New York: James Pott & Co., 1885.

2. P. M. Radford, "The Church of the Holy Trinity, Nashville."

Hunt, Mary Elizabeth. "Leaves from an Old Diary." In *Christ Church, Nashville, 1829–1929*, pp. 90–109. Anne Rankin, editor in chief. Nashville: Marshall & Bruce, 1929.

Nashville *Banner*, August 10, 1930.

Nashville *Banner*, May 7, 1952.

Nashville *Banner*, June 22, 1955.

Noll, Arthur H. *History of the Church in the Diocese of Tennessee*. New York: James Pott & Co., 1900.

Sewanee, Tennessee. Dupont Library, University of the South. Archives and Special Collections. "The Church of the Holy Trinity, Nashville," by P. M. Radford.

Stromquist, Victor H. "Church of the Holy Trinity." Unpublished inventory form prepared by Stromquist on October 1, 1956, in his capacity as Preservation Officer of the local A.I.A. chapter.

Tennessee. Davidson County. Register's Office.

Withey, Henry F., and Elsie R. Withey. *Biographical Dictionary of American Architects (Deceased)*. Los Angeles: New Age Publishing Co., 1956.

Wooldridge, John, editor. *History of Nashville, Tennessee*. Nashville: H. W. Crew, 1890.

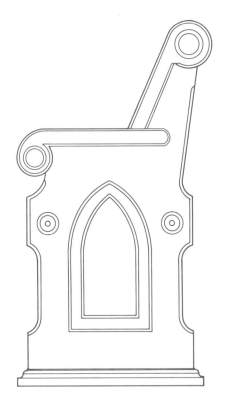

Pew Detail

Holy Trinity Episcopal Church
Nashville

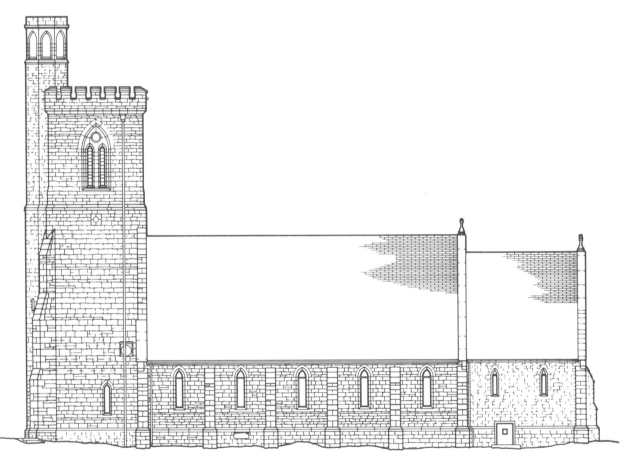

West Elevation
HABS drawing by Robert J. Dunay, 1970

Window Detail

The University of Nashville

(The Children's Museum)

THE Main Building of the University of Nashville, at 724 Second Avenue, South, was erected in 1853 to house the university's Literary Department. It was one of the first permanent structures of higher learning in the city. A two-story building of native gray limestone, it inaugurated the rich tradition of collegiate Gothic architecture in Nashville. Designed by Maj. Adolphus Heiman, one of the area's pioneer architects, the completed building was formally dedicated on October 4, 1854.

The University of Nashville was one of the pioneer educational institutions in Tennessee, its ancestry antedating Tennessee's statehood. Chartered in 1785 by the State of North Carolina as Davidson Academy, the institution was renamed Cumberland College in 1806. In 1816, the college suspended operation. It was reopened in 1824, under the presidency of Philip Lindsley, formerly of the College of New Jersey; and in 1826, the name was changed to the University of Nashville. The school remained a liberal arts college until 1850, when President Lindsley resigned and operations were suspended, pending the building of a new plant on a new site, the present location of the Main Building.

In 1851, a group of Nashville physicians leased the college buildings and opened a Medical Department of the University of Nashville. The Medical Department was successful from its beginning.

The Literary Department was reopened in 1854 in the new building designed by Heiman on the new campus, part of a tract of land purchased from Henry Middleton Rutledge in 1825.[1]

With this move, the University of Nashville diversified its curriculum and added professional training, thus assuming more of the characteristics of a true university. This attempt soon failed, however, when the entire faculty resigned in February of 1885. At this time, John Berrien Lindsley, Philip Lindsley's son, was named Chancellor, and the Literary Department was joined with the Western Military Institute.

This institution flourished on the campus until the Civil War, when the buildings of the University of Nashville were used by Federal authorities as a military hospital and barracks.

In 1867, the University of Nashville opened a preparatory school. The curriculum was soon expanded to include two years of college. From 1870 to 1875, the Main Building housed the Medical College, which had continued holding regular sessions throughout the Civil War. In 1875, the Peabody State Normal School was established at the university, and from that time until 1910, the Main Building was known as "Peabody College." By 1909, however, the Peabody governing board had determined to apply its funds to the establishment of George Peabody College for Teachers and had fixed its location by charter to lie near Vanderbilt University. The campus and buildings of the University of Nashville were thus conveyed by the Trustees of Peabody College in 1910 to Vanderbilt University, in exchange for land adjacent to the Vanderbilt campus.

From 1911 until it was relocated on the main Vanderbilt campus in 1925, the Vanderbilt School of Medicine used the old Main Building. Vanderbilt kept the property until the city of Nashville acquired it through condemnation proceedings in 1939. The city contemplated razing the Main Building, but the Tennessee Historical Society was successful in preserving it, and in 1945, after the building was restored, it became the quarters of the Children's Museum.

The building's foundations are stone, with brick piers supporting the central hall space and the four fireplaces. The walls are of gray limestone. A parapet wall along the roof line is brattished battlement, except over the entry vestibule, where it is simply corniced.

The vestibule doorway, 14 feet high, had a stone hood-mould over the double doors. Wood tracery above extended to the tudor-arched stone architrave. The doors to the vestibule central hall space have been replaced with iron

1. Allen Kelton, "The University of Nashville, 1850–1875," p. 455.

80 gates from the old university entrance. Marble flooring is used in the entry vestibule. Tile floors appear in the central hall, and the rest of the flooring is narrow hardwood.

The second-floor window of the vestibule is stone-plate tracery, with stone hood-mould.

Hipped roofs intersect at various levels, with the central hall as the highest point and the two symmetrical wings the lowest.

No records are available on the numerous stages of remodeling and alterations which have surely been made to the building. The only alterations about which anything is known are those made to the interior to accommodate the Children's Museum. A wing was also added to the rear of the building. Recent additions to site and surroundings include a sizable children's theater to the northwest of the Main Building and a large display area to the northeast. Both are one-story structures. Two smaller structures are attached to the southeast corner: a workshop and basement stair egress.

BIBLIOGRAPHY

Clayton, W. W. *History of Davidson County, Tennessee.* Philadelphia: J. W. Lewis, 1880.

Crabb, Alfred Leland. *Nashville: Personality of a City.* Indianapolis and New York: Bobbs-Merrill, 1960.

Frank, John G. "Adolphus Heiman: Architect and Soldier." *Tennessee Historical Quarterly*, V (March 1946), 35–57.

"The Historical Background of Peabody College." *Bulletin of George Peabody College for Teachers*, XXX (October 1941).

"Historical News and Notices." *Tennessee Historical Quarterly*, II (March 1943), 90.

"Historical News and Notices." *Tennessee Historical Quarterly*, IV (December 1945), 365–366.

Front Elevation

Kelton, Allen. "The University of Nashville, 1850–1875."
Ph.D. dissertation, George Peabody College for
Teachers, 1969.

Mahoney, Nell Savage. "Towers and Turrets: The
University of Nashville." Nashville *Tennessean
Magazine*, December 9, 1951, p. 26.

Merriam, Lucius S. *Higher Education in Tennessee.*
No. 16 in Contributions to American Educational
History series. Washington, D.C.: Government
Printing Office, 1893.

Nashville, Tennessee. Tennessee State Library and
Archives. Manuscripts Division. *University of
Nashville Records, 1852–1906*, vol. II. Minutes of the
Board of Trustees of the University of Nashville,
1852–1906.

University of Nashville. *Annual Announcement of the
Law, Literary, and Medical Departments of the
University of Nashville. Session of 1854–55.* Nashville:
Nashville Medical Journal, 1854.

University of Nashville. *Catalogue of the Literary and
Medical Department of the University of Nashville:
1858–59.* Nashville: John T. S. Fall, 1859.

University of Nashville. *Catalogue of the Officers and
Students of the Literary Department of the University
of Nashville for the Session of 1870–71.* Nashville:
Paul & Tavel, July 1871.

University of Nashville, Collegiate Department and
Western Military Institute. *The Official Register of
Cadets and Students for the Collegiate Year 1855–56
and Rules and Regulations with Annual
Announcements of Faculty and Officers for 1856–57.*
Nashville: Cameron & Fall, 1856.

Tennessee. Davidson County. Register's Office.

Wooldridge, John, editor. *History of Nashville,
Tennessee.* Nashville: H. W. Crew, 1890.

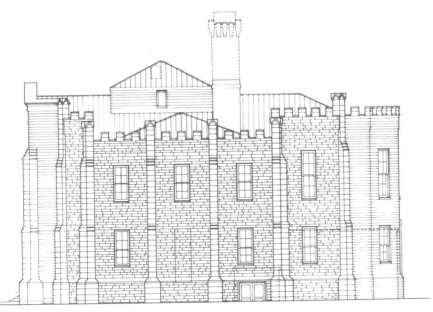

Side Elevation

Jubilee Hall, Fisk University

JUBILEE HALL, the oldest and largest building at Fisk University in Nashville, is the oldest permanent building for the higher education of Negroes in the United States. Completed in 1876, the L-shaped Victorian Gothic structure was designed by Stephen D. Hatch of New York.

Jubilee Hall was built with money raised by Fisk University's first group of Jubilee Singers, for whom it was named. It was designed for ultimate use as a women's dormitory, but the university's need for new buildings was so severe when it was completed that it was, according to an early contemporary account, made to answer all purposes.

Fisk University began in 1866 as the Fisk School, a free school for blacks in Nashville, providing instruction at all levels from the primary grades to normal school, with the training of properly qualified black teachers as one of its aims. It was founded by the American Missionary Association of New York and the Western Freedmen's Aid Commission of Cincinnati, assisted by General Clinton B. Fisk, assistant commissioner of the Freedmen's Bureau for Tennessee and Kentucky. Its campus was a group of old buildings formerly used as a government "railroad hospital," located on a block of privately owned land. Funds from the Missionary Association and the Freedmen's Bureau bought the land at $16,000; and through the efforts of General Fisk, for whom the school was gratefully named, the buildings were turned over to the Association for educational purposes.

Fisk School was chartered as a university in 1867. Funds for its support were scarce. By 1871, the institution had become heavily indebted; its old buildings were in an advanced state of disrepair. New buildings and a larger campus were badly needed. George L. White, Fisk's treasurer and music teacher, at this point organized a trial tour of student singers in an attempt to raise money for the school. The chorus of seven women and four men students made an extensive tour of the northern United States, Europe, and the British Isles. It was not until they had toured for some weeks that the group acquired a name: White decided to call them the Jubilee Singers, after the year of jubilee mentioned in the Old Testament, in which the Jews were delivered from bondage. Their singing of Negro spirituals was enthusiastically received, and the proceeds of the tour amounted to more than $150,000, enough to repay the purchase price of the university campus and to build Jubilee Hall.

On completion, Jubilee Hall stood six stories tall, including basement and cellar, and contained 120 rooms. The main entrance, facing south, was approached by a stone stairway with pillars supporting a small stone balcony. The massive front door was of black walnut with bronze trim. The front halls and stairways were wainscotted with alternating light and dark wood brought from the Mendi Mission in West Africa. The rest of the wainscotting throughout the building, together with doors, door facings, and cornices, was of white pine. The newel post of the main stairway in the front hall was composed of twenty-nine different kinds of fine cabinet wood.

On the first floor were reception rooms, assembly room, parlor, library, music room, dressing rooms for visitors and transient guests, and a dining room capable of seating 300. The upper floors were dormitory rooms, containing furniture of solid black walnut.

The building had steam heat, fire extinguishers on each floor, and hot and cold running water from three attic tanks filled from the five cisterns in the cellar which held 25,000 barrels of water and constituted Jubilee Hall's entire water supply.

The only substantial alteration to the building about which anything is known was made in 1965, when the interior was rebuilt to provide modern dormitory facilities. The exterior was preserved substantially as it had been prior to renovation, with these modifications: dormer windows were bricked up on the southeast corner and end pavilions; the central windows on the first and second floors of the rear façade were bricked over; fire escapes were removed, and new stone porches were built for the north, east, and west entrances.

Victorian Gothic dominates the landscape.

Jubilee Hall, Fisk University
Nashville

BIBLIOGRAPHY

Clayton, W. W. "Fisk University." In *History of Davidson County, Tennessee, with Illustrations and Biographical Sketches of Its Prominent Men*, by W. W. Clayton, pp. 260–262. Philadelphia: J. W. Lewis & Co., 1880.

Eaton, James N. "The Life of Erastus Milo Cravath." Master's thesis, Fisk University, 1959.

Federal Writers' Project. "Fisk University." In *Tennessee: A Guide to the State*, pp. 203–204. New York: Viking Press, 1939.

Fisk University. "After Forty Years: The Jubilee Singers." *Fisk University News*, II, No. 5 (October 1911).

Fisk University. *Catalogues of Fisk University, 1876–1880.* Nashville, 1876–1880.

"Fisk University." In *History of the American Missionary Association: Its Churches and Educational Institutions Among the Freedmen, Indians, and Chinese.* New York: S. W. Green, 1874.

Fisk University. History, Building and Site, and Services of Dedication at Nashville, Tennessee, January 1st, 1876. New York: Trustees of Fisk University, 1876.

Hopkins, Alphonso A. *The Life of Clinton Bowen Fisk.* New York: Funk and Wagnalls, 1910.

Marsh, J. B. I., editor. *The Story of the Jubilee Singers.* London: Hodder and Stoughton, 1877.

Moore, John T., and Austin P. Foster, editors. "Erastus Milo Cravath." In *Tennessee, the Volunteer State, 1769–1923*, IV, 723–724. Nashville: S. J. Clark, 1923.

Nashville, Tennessee. Fisk University. Main Library. "Fisk University. An Informal History of a People in Transition. In *News and Views, 1866–1954*, edited by Leslie Collins. Nashville, 1954.

New Orleans, Louisiana. American Missionary Association Archives. Amistad Research Center. Dillard University. Correspondence of Thomas C. Stewart, Superintendent of Construction for Jubilee Hall (1872–1875).

Pike, Gustavus D. *Singing Campaign for Ten Thousand Pounds.* New York: American Missionary Association, 1875.

Richardson, Joe M. "Fisk University: The First Critical Years." *Tennessee Historical Quarterly*, XXIX (Spring 1970), 24–41.

Strieby, M. E. "Jubilee Hall." *American Missionary*, XVII (March 1873), 50–52.

Taylor, Alnitheus A. *The Negro in Tennessee, 1865–1880.* Washington, D.C.: The Associated Publishers, 1941.

Tennessee. Davidson County. Register's Office.

Tipton, C. Robert. "The Fisk Jubilee Singers." *Tennessee Historical Quarterly*, XXIX (Spring 1970), 42–48.

Quiet interior space complements exterior complexity.

Vanderbilt University Gymnasium

THE "Old Gymnasium" of Vanderbilt University, now the Fine Arts Building, stands at West End and Twenty-third avenues. It is currently used as a fine arts museum and instruction center.

Vanderbilt University was chartered originally in 1872 as the Central University by the Methodist Episcopal Church, South, under whose control it operated until 1914. The name, however, was changed in 1873, when Methodist Bishop Holland N. McTyeire—who later became first President of the Vanderbilt University Board of Trust—secured from Cornelius Vanderbilt of New York an endowment for the university amounting to $500,000, subsequently increased to $1,000,000.

Completed in 1880, the Vanderbilt Gymnasium, with its considerable gymnastic equipment and indoor running track, was one of the earliest, best-equipped gymnasiums in the South. The interior was completely renovated for its present use in 1962. The exterior of the striking building preserves the rich Victorian architectural character of the early Vanderbilt campus; it is one of the few major buildings from the period to survive.

Its construction was made possible by William H. Vanderbilt, Cornelius Vanderbilt's eldest son. After his father's death in 1877, William Vanderbilt became the university's principal patron. In July 1879, he promised to give $100,000—a sum later increased to $150,000—for the purpose of erecting three new buildings on the campus: the Gymnasium, Science Hall, and Wesley Hall.

The *Announcement of Vanderbilt University, 1879–1880* (p. 23) provides an interesting contemporary description of the Gymnasium upon its completion:

The gymnasium is a brick building, 90 by 60 feet, of handsome architectural design, and substantial. It has a basement containing dressing and bath-rooms, and rooms for exercise, a principal floor for general exercise and training, and visitors' galleries accessible from the exterior by winding stairways in two of the towers.

The principal story is a single room for general exercise, 80 by 40 feet, with the ceiling 32 feet high. It contains a running and walking track, and a complete equipment of gymnastic apparatus, comprising rowing machines, chest-expanders, parallel and horizontal ladders, springboards, Indian clubs, dumb-bells, etc.

Peter J. Williamson, assumed to have been the architect of the gymnasium, was one of the pioneer architects in Nashville. He came to the United States from Holland before the Civil War, settled in Wisconsin, and volunteered in the Federal Army, winning the rank of major before the war ended. He subsequently settled in Nashville, where he became a member of the firm of Dobson and Williamson. He was also the architect for Science Hall and Wesley Hall at Vanderbilt.

Absurdly out of scale with the huge new dormitory, Carmichael Towers, nearby, the Old Gym still stands proudly as a landmark on West End Avenue. It has long been the butt of jokes made about "Methodist Gothic" and "Nashville Norman," but it is a rich inheritance from an era which valued both the expressive and the functional in its buildings.

Given the form of a chapel in high Victorian style, the Old Gym, completed in 1880, was one of the first university structures dedicated to physical culture.

Vanderbilt University Gymnasium
Nashville

88

BIBLIOGRAPHY

Clayton, W. W. "Vanderbilt University." In *History of Davidson County, Tennessee, with Illustrations and Biographical Sketches of Its Prominent Men*, by W. W. Clayton. Philadelphia: J. W. Lewis & Co., 1880.

Federal Writers' Project. *Tennessee: A Guide to the State*. New York: Viking Press, 1939.

Insurance Maps of Nashville, Tennessee, vol. 4, Plate 496. New York: Sanborn Map Co., 1914.

[McGaw, Robert A.] "The Old Gym." In *A Selection of New Works by Nashville Artists*. Catalogue for the first exhibition at the Vanderbilt Art Gallery, February 4–25, 1962.

Mims, Edwin. *History of Vanderbilt University*. Nashville: Vanderbilt University Press, 1946.

Nashville, Tennessee. Joint University Libraries. "Views of the [Vanderbilt] Campus" Collection.

Nashville, Tennessee. Joint University Libraries. Special Collection. The John James Tigert Papers, 1824–1957.

Tennessee. Davidson County. Chancery Court Minute Book "W," p. 267.

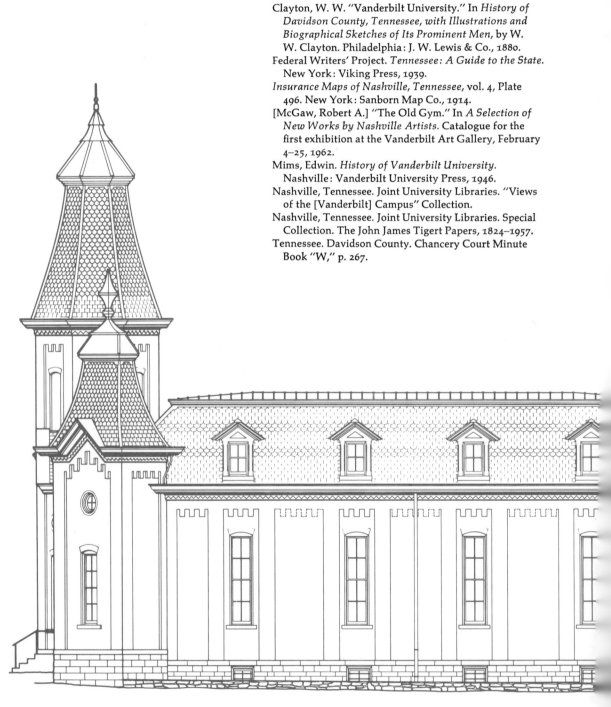

Northwest Elevation

Tennessee. Davidson County. Chancery Court Minute
Book "X," p. 309.
Vanderbilt University. *Announcement of Vanderbilt
University, 1879–1880.* Nashville: 1880.
Wooldridge, John, editor. *History of Nashville,
Tennessee.* Nashville: H. W. Crew, 1890.

Vanderbilt University Gymnasium
Nashville

Complicated truss work allowed the creation of an open gymnasium floor space without posts.

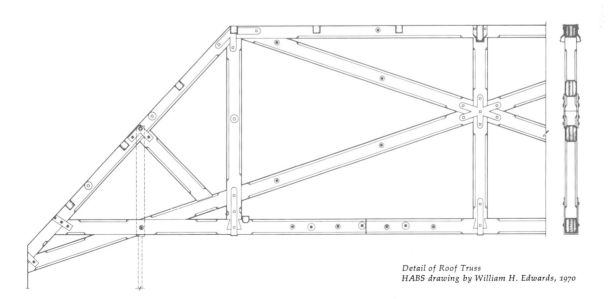

Detail of Roof Truss
HABS drawing by William H. Edwards, 1970

West Side Row, Vanderbilt University

THESE five two-story brick buildings erected in 1886 and 1887 on the Vanderbilt University campus in Nashville represent an early venture in student housing. They were built at a time when residence on campus for university students was not the customary thing it later became. They were made possible by a gift of $10,000 from William H. Vanderbilt, son of Commodore Cornelius Vanderbilt, whose initial gift of a million dollars built and endowed the university.

When Vanderbilt University opened for classes in October 1875, there were no dormitories: the school's governing board considered them to be "injurious to morals and manners." Within three years, however, the Board of Trust recognized the need for student housing, and, for $1,500, the Executive Committee bought a strip of land adjoining the university grounds on the west. On June 14, 1886, Methodist Bishop Holland N. McTyeire, President of the Vanderbilt Board of Trust and the man entrusted by Cornelius Vanderbilt with establishing the university, reported to the Board of Trust receipt of a check for $10,000 from William H. Vanderbilt, "to be used at my discretion, for the library or for other University interests. . . . it was thought best to build four dormitories on the Western part of the campus, accommodating sixty-four students."[1]

The buildings were designed and their construction was supervised by Oliver H. Landruth, Professor of Civil Engineering at Vanderbilt, who received $500 for his work.

The four brick buildings completed in 1886 were identical, each with two stories containing eight rooms and housing sixteen men. No two rooms connected; all had outside entrances. Exterior wrought-iron stairways, one on either side, led to the upper level of each building. One large center chimney, with eight flues, serving the eight fireplaces inside, was a distinctive feature of each building. The structures were named Alpha, Bellevue, Cumberland, and Delphi.

The following year, two more identical dormitories were built, named Euclid and Franklin, and work was begun on a dining room.

These six buildings continued as dormitories until 1956, when they were converted to offices or apartments. Alpha was torn down in 1966 to make room for Carmichael Towers, a new men's dormitory, but the remaining five survive, as does the dining hall, which is of different design and is now the Naval ROTC Building. The buildings preserve their original appearance and form, although connecting doors and other modifications have been made inside to adapt the space to modern use. The buildings are now used for the Vanderbilt Housing Office, apartments, the Student Association, the Cultural Affairs Council, and the office of Vanderbilt University Press.

BIBLIOGRAPHY

Mims, Edwin. *History of Vanderbilt University*. Nashville: Vanderbilt University Press, 1946.

Nashville, Tennessee. Joint University Libraries. Special Collection. The John James Tigert Papers, 1824–1957.

Nashville, Tennessee. Joint University Libraries. Vanderbilt University Archives. "Seventy Years After," by Owen H. Wilson.

Vanderbilt University. *Announcements for Vanderbilt University*, 1878–1956.

Vanderbilt University. Board of Trust. Minutes, vols. I and II.

1. Vanderbilt University, Board of Trust, Minutes, vols. I and II, pp. 142, 450, 495.

West Side Row, Vanderbilt University
Nashville

An elaborate Tudor-style chimney served eight fireplaces which in turn warmed sixteen students.

Rock Castle

ROCK CASTLE, three quarters of a mile east of Hendersonville on Indian Lake Road in Sumner County, represents a transitional element in frontier Tennessee architecture. It was built in the late 1700s by Gen. Daniel Smith, on a land grant of 3,140 acres given him for service in the Revolutionary War. Rock Castle is reminiscent of the simple homes of the Eastern Seaboard, from which General Smith came to Tennessee. It was the first of three Middle Georgian stone houses built in Sumner County and is among the first important houses in the state to reflect a measure of architectural planning.

Owned by the State of Tennessee since 1969, Rock Castle is presently under consideration as a museum and research center.

The house was presumably designed by General Smith himself, although no plans have been found; and Smith's substantial library is not known to have contained any architectural or pattern books.

A native Virginian, Smith was a graduate of William and Mary College and a surveyor by profession. Thomas Jefferson said of him that "Daniel Smith was a practical surveyor, whose work never needed correction. For intelligence, well-cultivated talents, for integrity, and usefulness, in soundness of judgment . . . he was equalled by few men."[1] At the end of the Revolutionary War, Smith settled in what is now Sumner County. He was appointed surveyor in 1783 to lay out the town of Nashville. He served as trustee of Davidson Academy, the first institution of learning chartered in the Cumberland country; and he was a member of the North Carolina Convention which ratified the U.S. Constitution in 1789. When President Washington appointed William Blount governor of the Territory of the United States South of the Ohio River, Daniel Smith was made secretary. He was frequently acting governor in Blount's absence from the territory. Smith was the first person to publish a map of Tennessee, which he made from his own surveys. In 1796, Smith was chairman of the committee charged with drafting the first constitution of the State of Tennessee. Appointed in 1798 to fill out Andrew Jackson's unexpired U.S. Senate term, following Jackson's resignation, Smith was elected U.S. Senator again in 1805 and served until 1809.

It is generally agreed that General Smith started construction of Rock Castle in 1784, although there is no primary documentation for this date. The house was constructed of native gray limestone quarried a few hundred yards from the building site.[2] An almost virgin forest surrounded the area, and it is probable that the lumber used was cut there. Joists and rafters of oak and cedar were used, the rafters being marked on each side with roman numerals made by straight saw cuts, indicating that they were cut and fitted on the ground.

Construction was slow: there were problems with Indians, a lack of skilled workmen, and a scarcity of proper building materials. In 1793, Mrs. Smith wrote to her husband that the builder had stopped sawing wood for the interior and that Indians were still making trouble. On the same day, July 20, the builder also wrote to Smith, reporting that the walls were about one foot above the window sills, that frames for the first floor were in, and that he was working on assorted joists, lintels, and window frames.[3] The exact date on which the house was completed is unknown, and the first reference to Rock Castle as habitable is found in Governor John Sevier's journal, where he records arriving there on May 24, 1797, and staying the night.

Smith's sister, Mrs. Peter Hansborough, had two sons, Peter and Smith, who came to Sumner County from Philadelphia to work on their

---

1. Kenneth McKellar, *Tennessee Senators as Seen by One of Their Successors*, p. 113.

2. "Rock Castle," *American Historical Magazine*, V, No. 4 (October 1900), 293.
3. *Ibid.*, p. 200. See also Daniel Smith Papers, Tennessee Historical Society, Tennessee State Library and Archives.

Meticulously cut stone formed a bastion against the wilderness.

Rock Castle
Hendersonville

uncle's house.[4] Correspondence between Smith Hansborough and General Smith indicates that the former was in charge of construction and served as a carpenter on the job. The Hansboroughs recruited local help, and a William Stamp is known to have worked on the stone walls. A descendant of General Smith remembers hearing that the original stonemasons and carpenters were from Philadelphia, but that they were all killed by Indians and that their replacements were less skilled local tradesmen.[5]

4. Joseph D. Delaney, "A Historical Study of Rock Castle," p. 14.
5. Interview, Miss Sarah C. Berry.

The house is L-shaped, two stories tall, and was framed with hand-hewn trusses, notched and pegged. There are chimneys at the east and west ends of the original structure and one large chimney over the kitchen wing. Interior downstairs walls with fireplaces all had a central mantel, overmantel, and side cabinets, set within an integrated wood-paneled wall. Most of the interior woodwork, including the paneling, is of black walnut. A special decorative feature is the chair rail

Vertical Section
HABS drawing by Robert J. Dunay, 1970
Traced from measured drawings by Cooper and Warterfield, Architects

The nearby forest provided lumber for the heavy timbers.

100 throughout. Door and window architraves were of hewn poplar. Roof shingles were riven of cedar.[6] The hinges are a notable feature: they are an **H-L** type, with small square leather washers between heads and hinge.

Sometime between 1825 and 1849, during the lifetime of General Smith's son George, the exterior of the house was remodeled. Reflecting the growing taste for Greek revival architecture, a wooden front porch was added.[7] A porch at the rear, since replaced by a facsimile in stone, was presumably added at the same time. In 1886, the original cedar shingles were replaced by a slate roof, causing the rafters to bend under its weight. Electricity was installed in the 1940s.[8]

In 1953, during construction of the Tennessee Valley Authority's Old Hickory Lock and Dam on the Cumberland River, much of the Smith land was condemned and flooded. At this time, the floor of the basement, originally tamped earth, was done over with concrete, and concrete box staircases were added to the two basement entrances.

In 1959, the rear upstairs bedroom in the leg of the ell was renovated, and gypsum board was placed over the original plaster walls. In 1964, a stone slab porch with wooden roof replaced the old one. The louvered shutters on the house are not original; they may have been installed around the middle of the nineteenth century. It is likely that the original shutters were solid wood panels, offering better protection from Indian attacks.

There were at least five outbuildings on the estate: a spring house, smokehouse, carriage house, and slaves' quarters. Of these, only the smokehouse has survived. It stands south of the dwelling, within 35 feet of the shoreline of Old Hickory Lake.

---

6. Walter T. Durham, *The Great Leap Westward: A History of Sumner County, Tennessee, from Its Beginnings to 1805*, pp. 137–139.

7. Delaney, "A Historical Study of Rock Castle," p. 31.

8. Interview, Miss Sarah C. Berry.

BIBLIOGRAPHY

Albright, Edward. *Early History of Middle Tennessee*. Nashville: Brandon Printing Co., 1908.

Brandau, Roberta S., editor. *History of Homes and Gardens of Tennessee*. Nashville: Parthenon Press, 1936.

Bryant, Gladys E. "Daniel Smith, Citizen of the Tennessee Frontier." Master's thesis, Vanderbilt University, 1960.

Burke, Pauline W. *Emily Donelson of Tennessee*. 2 vols. Richmond, Va.: Garrett and Massie, 1941.

Carr, John. *Early Times in Middle Tennessee*. Nashville: E. Stevenson and F. A. Owen, 1857.

Cisco, Jay Guy. *Historic Sumner County, Tennessee*. Nashville: Folk-Keelin Printing Co., 1909.

Delaney, Joseph D. "A Historical Study of Rock Castle." Nashville: Tennessee Historical Commission, 1970.

Dewitt, John H., editor. "Journal of Governor John Sevier, 1790–1815." *Tennessee Historical Magazine*, VI (April 1920), 18–60.

Durham, Walter T. *The Great Leap Westward: A History of Sumner County, Tennessee, From Its Beginnings to 1805*. Nashville: Parthenon Press, 1969.

Federal Writers' Project. *Tennessee: A Guide to the State*. New York: Viking Press, 1939.

Garrett, William R., and Albert V. Goodpasture. *History of Tennessee*. Nashville: Brandon Printing Co., 1903.

McKellar, Kenneth. *Tennessee Senators as Seen by One of Their Successors*. Kingsport, Tenn.: Southern Publishers, 1942.

"Papers of General Daniel Smith." *American Historical Magazine*, VI (July 1901), 213–235.

"Rock Castle." *American Historical Magazine*, V (October 1900), 292–295.

Nashville, Tennessee. Manuscripts Division. Tennessee State Library and Archives. Box S. I, No. 93 S. Tennessee Historical Society. Daniel Smith Papers.

Tennessee. Sumner County. County Court Clerk's Office.

Tennessee. Sumner County. Register's Office.

The stairwell is reminiscent of colonial East Coast architecture.

The Hays-Kiser House

THE Hays-Kiser house at 834 Reeves Road, near Antioch, was begun prior to 1796 for Charles Hays (1777–1854). According to family descendants, Charles's father, John Hays of Sampson County, North Carolina, came to Tennessee with skilled workmen and stayed to supervise construction of the house until it was completed. A document in the family, now lost, described the work in progress during the fall of 1795. It commented on the fine quality of clay available for brick-making at the site but expressed concern about the possibility of finishing one brick room with a lean-to for the slaves before the onset of winter. Presumably, the house was finished prior to the marriage of Charles Hays to Ann Blackman in 1797.

Designed in a severe and unornamented version of the Federal style, the original structure was of Flemish-bonded brick with white painted wood trim. In 1797, it consisted of one large and one smaller room on each of its two floors, with a one-room ell to the north of the smaller first-floor room. Sometime later, a room above the ell was added, opening onto an upstairs gallery added at the same time. This gallery was removed early in the twentieth century to make room for the present two-story frame addition. Now gone also is the kitchen-dining room building, originally west of the house and connected to it by a louvred passage. This passage was sometimes referred to as a ballroom, as it was 60 feet long.

The glory of the house has always been its handsome woodwork, embracing the "chip, gouge, and drill" technique of carving associated with German workmen. The woodwork in the master bedroom upstairs preserves its original finish of fake graining in imitation of mahogany and green marble.

Charles Hays is referred to in Clayton's *History of Davidson County* as "a Christian gentleman and founder of the Baptist Church at Antioch." He was a generous benefactor to the community and a large landholder, owning some 2,500 acres of fertile Mill Creek land. He gave land for a school, for the Baptist Church, and for the Antioch Temperance Society.

On Charles Hays's death in 1854, the house passed to a grandson and in 1870 it was sold to Peter Rieves. It remained in the hands of Rieves descendants until acquired by Mr. and Mrs. John Kiser in 1966.

BIBLIOGRAPHY

Clayton, W. W. *History of Davidson County, Tennessee, with Illustrations and Biographical Sketches of Its Prominent Men.* Philadelphia: J. W. Lewis & Co., 1880.

Hays-Kiser House
Antioch

Paneling is a surprising touch in an eighteenth-century Tennessee country farmhouse.

Travellers' Rest

THE site for Travellers' Rest, 6.7 miles southwest of Nashville, on what is now Farrell Parkway, was bought by Judge John Overton, one of Nashville's first lawyers, in 1796, the year Tennessee became a state. Construction of the house that he was to call Travellers' Rest began three years later.

John Overton, who came to the Cumberland country from Virginia and Kentucky, had been appointed Territorial Revenue Collector of the area when it was still the Mero District of North Carolina. He became a close friend and advisor of Andrew Jackson, grew to be a distinguished Tennessee jurist, and, with Jackson, founded the city of Memphis.

Travellers' Rest remained in the Overton family until 1938, when Jacob McGavock Dickinson, great-grandson of Judge Overton, sold the estate to Dr. John B. Youmans. The Louisville and Nashville Railroad Company bought the place in 1951. In 1954, the railroad gave to the National Society of Colonial Dames of America in Tennessee the three acres on which the house stands. The society conducted extensive restoration of the property and now operates the estate and the house as a museum.

Travellers' Rest evolved between 1799 and 1885, in three distinct stages: Federal (1799–1812); Greek revival (1828); and Victorian (1885).

The original section of Travellers' Rest, built in 1799, was a simple two-story, four-room Federal clapboard house with hewn-log frame construction and a stone cellar. A two-story, two-room addition was made in 1812, and the resulting six-room block completed the simple Federal house initially built.

Sometime between 1821 and 1829, a long two-story, eight-room Greek-revival ell was added to the Federal block. At the same time, Overton built a carriage house and more cabins for his slaves. In 1887, a two-room Victorian addition to the ell was built.

Although no architect is known to have participated in any of the three stages of construction, something is known of the builders. Two carpenters, David Cumming and Frederick Pinkley, were hired by Judge Overton to construct the initial four-room house. They were to hew the corner posts, sills, sleepers, and other heavy timbers, as well as to produce the clapboards and rive the shingles. For this, Overton agreed to sell them 320 acres of land on Stone's River for two dollars an acre.[1]

The exterior walls of Travellers' Rest are of beaded weatherboarding. Outbuildings, including Judge Overton's law office, a smokehouse, and a slave house, were of brick.

The house has clearly undergone numerous stages of extensive remodeling and alteration through the years. It is likely that its appearance was altered, during each of the two major additions, to conform to contemporary style, but little documentation exists to unravel these various undertakings and the extent to which they modified the original house.

The present owners, the Colonial Dames, undertook two major restoration projects. Since the original two-story, four-room building had been so extensively remodeled and added to, the decision about what to restore was difficult. The Colonial Dames decided to restore the house to its appearance in the early nineteenth century, the period within the lifetime of Judge John Overton, as a memorial to the man and as a portrait of life in those years.

The first restoration project, begun and completed in 1966, involved only the six rooms of the initial Federal part of the house. It was directed by Nashville architect Charles W. Warterfield Jr.

The second project, completed in 1970, involved the central or Greek-revival addition and was directed by Clinton E. Brush III, also of Nashville.

The 1885 Victorian addition was not made an integral part of the restoration. Instead, it was simply modified to accommodate facilities

1. Henry Lee Swint, "Travellers' Rest: Home of Judge John Overton," p. 123.

Chaste proportion is the bond between such country façades and the neoclassic taste of urban dwellings.

Travellers' Rest
Nashville

necessary to the current operation of Travellers' Rest as a museum.

The reports of the two architects conducting the restoration make clear that little of the original fabric of the house has survived. Much had previously been eliminated during early alterations, and little of what was left could be salvaged for re-use in the restoration. Many elements have been restored after careful, painstaking research, and where definitive documentation was not available, restoration has been done on the basis of comparable items known to have existed in the area during the appropriate period.

BIBLIOGRAPHY

Brandau, Roberta S., editor. *History of Homes and Gardens of Tennessee*. Nashville: Parthenon Press, 1936.

Caldwell, Mrs. James E. *Historic and Beautiful Country Homes Near Nashville, Tennessee*. Nashville: Brandon Printing Co., 1911.

Davis, Louise. "Travellers' Rest." Nashville *Tennessean Magazine*, April 8, 1956, pp. 20–21.

Federal Writers' Project. *Tennessee: A Guide to the State*. New York: Viking Press, 1939.

Swint, Henry Lee. "Travellers' Rest: Home of Judge John Overton." *Tennessee Historical Quarterly*, XXVI (Summer 1967), 119–136.

West Elevation
HABS drawing by Patrick W. Crawford, 1970
Traced from original drawings by Brush, Hutchison & Gwinn, Architects

The geometry of rails and siding is a foil to surrounding vegetation.

WINE CELLAR

Cragfont

CRAGFONT, seven miles east of Gallatin on Highway 25, is the largest and most architecturally refined of several native stone structures erected in Sumner County in the late eighteenth and early nineteenth centuries. It was built in 1802 as a home for Gen. James Winchester, who figured prominently in early Tennessee political and military affairs.

A T-shaped house of gray, rough-finished Tennessee limestone, Cragfont was described by a traveler through Tennessee in 1802:

> We . . . saw . . . General Winchester . . . at a stone house that was building for him on the road; this mansion, considering the country, bore the external marks of grandeur; it consisted of four large rooms on the ground floor, one story and a garrett. . . . The stones are of a chalky nature; there are no others in all that part of Tennessee except round flints. . . . The workmen employed to finish the inside came from Baltimore, a distance of nearly 700 miles. . . . There are so few of the inhabitants that build in this manner, masons being still scarcer than carpenters or joiners.[1]

The house stands two-and-a-half stories tall, with basement. Spaced across the front of the house between the first and second levels are four large six-pointed stars. Though decorative, the stars serve a utilitarian purpose: connected to iron rods within the thick stone walls, they serve as braces.[2] The house consists of a main block with a central hall flanked by one large room on the left of the entrance and two smaller rooms on the right, with the same arrangement on both floors. The central hall opens on a smaller hall to the rear, which, with the two rooms beyond it, forms the stem of the T. Experts in early construction methods believe that the first story of this wing to the rear was constructed at the same time as the main block of the house.

At some time before 1825, a second story of brick was added to the rear wing, and a two-story brick smokehouse was attached as part of the wing. Galleries were built on the east and west sides of the wing. Family history tells of a ball held in 1825 in the larger of the two upstairs rooms in the addition, honoring the visit of the Marquis de Lafayette.

When the house was sold out of the Winchester family, it passed through the hands of several subsequent owners and suffered more from neglect and poor maintenance than from alterations or additions. Over the years, the original front door was removed and replaced by a nondescript substitute, and the original windows were removed and larger ones out of keeping with the period were installed.

In 1958, the house and eleven acres surrounding it were bought by the State of Tennessee, and restoration was begun. The property is now a museum, restored, furnished, and maintained by the Sumner County Chapter of the Association for the Preservation of Tennessee Antiquities.

As restoration got under way, workmen discovered the old windows and copies of an original sash in the attic of the house. A new door in keeping with the style of Cragfont was designed by Nashville architect Clinton Parrent. A shingle roof replaced the tin one; and the dormer windows, which an investigation of the third-floor attic revealed to have been original to the house, were restored. The galleries, which had collapsed on the east and west sides of the north wing of the house, were restored, their appearance derived from remnants of the original structures. The house is now the subject of both constructional and historical research, as every effort is made to recreate its original appearance.

Gen. James Winchester, for whom Cragfont was built, was an officer in the Revolutionary War who came to Tennessee in 1785 and soon acquired extensive land holdings. President Washington appointed him as a member of the Legislative Council of the Southwest Territory

1. F. A. Michaux, *Travels to the Westward of the Allegheny Mountains in the States of Ohio, Kentucky, and Tennessee in the Year 1802*, p. 254.

2. Hugh Walker, "Follow a Buffalo Trail to Sumner Homes," Nashville *Tennessean*, April 21, 1968.

Cragfont
Gallatin

in 1794, and the following year, he became a brigadier general of the Mero (North Carolina) District, of which the Cumberland River country was a part. He was reappointed brigadier general in 1796 by Tennessee's first governor, John Sevier, and was also Speaker of the first Tennessee Senate. In 1819, he was appointed commissioner to determine and mark the boundary of West Tennessee. With Andrew Jackson, John Overton, and William Vaulx, Winchester helped to found the city of Memphis, whose development was his last major work. He died at Cragfont in 1826.

BIBLIOGRAPHY

Allen, Ward. "Cragfont: Grandeur on the Tennessee Frontier." *Tennessee Historical Quarterly*, XXIII (June 1964), 103–120.

Association for the Preservation of Tennessee Antiquities. Sumner County Chapter. Cragfont Files.

Brandau, Roberta Seawell. *History of Homes and Gardens of Tennessee.* Nashville: Parthenon Press, 1936.

Cisco, Jay Guy. *Historic Sumner County, Tennessee.* Nashville: Folk-Keelin Printing Co., 1909.

Cochran, Gifford A. *Grandeur in Tennessee.* New York: J. J. Augustin Publishers, 1946.

Durham, Walter T. *The Great Leap Westward: A History of Sumner County, Tennessee, From Its Beginnings to 1805.* Nashville: Parthenon Press, 1969.

Michaux, F. A. *Travels to the Westward of the Allegheny Mountains in the States of Ohio, Kentucky, and Tennessee in the Year 1802.* London: Printed by W. Flint for J. Mawman, 1805.

Moore, John Trotwood. *Tennessee, the Volunteer State,* vol. II. Nashville: S. J. Clarke Publishing Co., 1923.

Walker, Hugh. "On the Frozen River of Raisins, the Indians Won." Nashville *Tennessean*, December 22, 1968.

East Elevation
HABS drawing by Daryl P. Fortier, 1971

Stripped of ornament, the rear of the great house is a tribute to a builder's manipulation of mass and texture.

Cragfont
Gallatin

Once badly neglected, a venerable structure has been given new vitality through restoration.

Oaklands

OAKLANDS, now a municipal museum, was built in three successive stages, which present a continuum of architectural styles illustrating cultural life in Middle Tennessee during the nineteenth century.

No definite building dates are known, but the first house incorporated into the present structure is believed to date from around 1815. The second house was built about 1825; and about 1859 or 1860, a third section was built, creating the present house.

Oaklands faces south-southwest on a circular drive at the north end of Maney Avenue in Murfreesboro, about a mile north of the Rutherford County Courthouse. It was built on land granted in 1786 by the State of North Carolina to Ezekiel White, who sold 274 acres of it in 1798 to Col. Hardy Murfree. Colonel Murfree, for whom the city of Murfreesboro is named, eventually owned more than 40,000 acres of land in Tennessee. He died intestate in 1809, and the Tennessee Legislature passed an act in 1812 empowering the Court of Williamson County to appoint seven commissioners to make an equitable division of his lands among his heirs. The Ezekiel White tract was a part of the land allowed to one of his daughters, Sarah Hardy, who was married to Dr. James Maney.[1]

The first house on the property (first known as Maney's Grove, then Oak Manor, and finally as Oaklands)[2] thus may have been built for the Murfree heirs, but there is also the possibility that it was built for the Maney family. The second and third additions were known to have been built by Dr. James Maney.

The land remained the property of the Maney family until 1884. At James Maney's death in 1872, it was inherited by his son, Lewis Maney, and Lewis's wife. Lewis Maney died in 1882, and in 1884, Oaklands and 200 acres of land were sold at auction to settle his estate. Mrs. Elizabeth T. Swope bought the property. Her will in 1890 left it to her daughter, Mrs. George M. Darrow.

In 1912, the house and twenty-nine acres were sold for $18,000 to Mr. and Mrs. R. B. Roberts. In 1936, Mrs. Roberts, then a widow, sold the property to Albert Brevard Jetton and his sister, Rebecca Jetton. Miss Jetton survived her brother and sold the house and its twenty-nine remaining acres to the city of Murfreesboro in 1957. The acreage became a city park, and, in 1959, the house was deeded to the Oaklands Association, formed to restore and maintain the building and to open it to the public.

The house has been restored to what architectural and historical evidence indicate to have been its original plan and construction in 1860. Since it did evolve in three stages, its earlier appearances can best be understood by a study of its alterations.

The first house, facing east, consisted of two rooms, one above the other. Behind them was a kitchen connected to the main dwelling by a breeze-way or "dog-trot."[3]

The second house, facing south, was brick, with chimneys at the east and west ends and entrances on the south and east sides. This structure was added to the original building.

In the 1850s, two large rooms on the ground floor and halls upstairs and down were added to the south front of the house. The center front room of the second house was united with the new front hall and an elaborate semicircular staircase was built in it. To accommodate the higher ceilings of the addition and to correlate the lines of the exterior, the roof of the middle structure was raised about four feet.

During the occupation of Oaklands by the Darrow family, the front porch was built, probably about 1890 to 1900.

The house is approximately 73 by 62 feet, with 18-inch solid brick walls. The foundations are of Tennessee limestone. Wooden columns 12 inches square support the roof over the porch, and there are massive, elaborate cornices at the eaves. The six chimneys are of brick.

Although most of the house now has oak floors of recent origin, the original yellow

1. Robert M. McBride, "Oaklands: A Venerable Host; A Renewed Welcome," p. 305.
2. Ibid.
3. Ibid., p. 306.

Oaklands
Murfreesboro

118 poplar flooring, ranging in width from 6½ to 14 inches, is found in the side entry. The doors are nine feet tall, with recessed panels.

The house fell into neglect after it became vacant in the 1950s. It was vandalized, its windows and mantels broken or destroyed. Photographs of its condition when acquired by the Oaklands Association indicate its wreckage by 1959. The mantels in the house now are of the period of the house but are not original to it.

Oaklands was command headquarters for Col. William W. Duffield of the 9th Michigan Regiment, U.S.A., from March until May 1862, when Duffield left Murfreesboro for duty in Kentucky. He returned in July, with Union Gen. T. T. Crittenden, who was to be commander of the Murfreesboro garrison. On the morning after their arrival, Confederate Gen. Nathan Bedford Forrest staged a raid and captured Murfreesboro. The surrender of the Federal forces took place at Oaklands. For the next several months, the house was considered a post of the Confederate officers. Confederate Gen.

Braxton Bragg was a frequent visitor, as was Col. William Wirt Adams of Forrest's staff. Other notable guests were Jefferson Davis, President of the Confederacy, who arrived in Murfreesboro on December 12, 1862, for a stay of several days at the house; Maj. Gen. Leonidas Polk; and Brig. Gen. George E. Maney, a cousin of the owners of Oaklands.[4]

From the Battle of Murfreesboro—December 31, 1862, to January 2, 1863—until the end of the war, the city was under Federal occupation, and Oaklands served as headquarters for Union officers Maj. Gen. Thomas L. Crittenden and Brig. Gen. Horatio P. VanCleve.

BIBLIOGRAPHY

Hughes, Mary B. *Hearthstones*. 2d edition. Nashville: Mid-South Publishing Company, 1942.
McBride, Robert M. "Oaklands: A Venerable Host; A Renewed Welcome." *Tennessee Historical Quarterly*, XXII (December 1963), 303–322.
Tennessee. Rutherford County. Register of Deeds.

4. *Ibid.*, p. 317.

Italianate elegance was a final graft onto a succession of farmhouses.

Oaklands
Murfreesboro

Exuberant ornament was an expression of new wealth in the old South.

The Hermitage

THE Hermitage, home of Andrew Jackson, seventh president of the United States, is on Rachel's Lane, a half-mile west of Highway 70-N, approximately twelve miles east of Nashville.

The house and 500 acres of surrounding farmland were bought by the state of Tennessee for $48,000 in 1856, eleven years after Jackson's death, when the General's heir and adopted son, Andrew Jackson Jr., was forced by financial reverses to sell the property.

From 1856 until 1889, the state considered a number of proposals for the Hermitage. It was, for example, offered to the federal government as the site for a southern branch of the U.S. Military Academy—an offer that came to nothing in the gathering tension preceding the Civil War. The idea of selling the land in lots was discussed. In 1887, it was proposed that the Hermitage be made into a home for Confederate soldiers, a proposal taken seriously enough to prompt a small but determined group to form the Ladies Hermitage Association in 1888 as an emergency measure to save the property from misuse. The founders were Mrs. Andrew Jackson III, whose idea the association was; Andrew Jackson III; Mrs. D. R. Dorris; and Mr. and Mrs. William A. Donelson. The association was chartered on February 19, 1889, its objectives being to purchase the Hermitage and immediate grounds and maintain them in a manner befitting Jackson's memory. The Tennessee legislature in 1889 agreed to a compromise with the association, turning over to the group the Hermitage and 25 acres, on which a new building was to be erected as a Confederate soldiers' home. A series of legislative acts—in 1923, 1935, and 1960—turned over to the Ladies Hermitage Association the original 500 acres of Hermitage lands and 125 more, with the agreement that the Hermitage be preserved in perpetuity as a proper memorial.

The Hermitage is a house of stately simplicity. It stands back from the road about a hundred yards, a two-story brick building facing south, flanked by one-story wings on the east and west sides. The original drive leading to it—no longer used—is guitar-shaped and lined by craggy cedars whose planting Jackson supervised in 1837.

The foundations of the house are native limestone, quarried on the farm. The bricks for the walls were made on the place, from clay dug out of the field across the road. The original flooring remains throughout the house except for the floor in the dining room, which had to be replaced. All interior floors are wide poplar boards. Porch flooring is of Tennessee red cedar.[1]

The front of the house is painted white, to cover discoloration left by fire that gutted the building's interior in 1834. The brick walls of the sides and rear are unpainted.

A two-story portico with six modified Corinthian columns and a second-floor gallery extends across the main unit. The front portico is floored with flagstones of Tennessee limestone.

The wings, built when the main building was enlarged in 1831, extend 9 feet in front of the central unit. The west wing contains dining room and pantry, with a passage leading to the semi-detached kitchen. A feature of the dining room fireplace is the "Eighth-of-January" mantelpiece, a rustic affair built of pieces of rough hickory by one of Jackson's veterans of the Battle of New Orleans. He made it singlehandedly, working only on successive anniversaries of the battle until he finished it, January 8, 1839. It was installed on January 8, 1840.[2]

In the west wing are the library/office, the overseer's room, and the side entrance on the east.

From the front portico, double front doors with fanlight and sidelights lead into a wide central hall running from front to back. The graceful spiral staircase suspended from the rear wall is the hall's most striking feature. Much

1. Stanley F. Horn, *The Hermitage: Home of Old Hickory*, pp. 60–61.
2. *Ibid.*, p. 60.

The Hermitage
Nashville

has been written about the wallpaper in this hall—pictorial wallpaper which Jackson ordered from France in 1835, showing scenes from the legend of Telemachus in search of his father Ulysses. The set of 25 strips in the Hermitage hall is one of the few sets of historic scenic papers preserved in this country.[3]

The upstairs floor plan is similar to that downstairs: a broad central hall running the full length of the house, with two bedrooms on either side and doors at front and rear opening onto the upstairs front and back porticoes.

The back portico differs from the front in having a higher foundation, Doric columns, and a Doric pediment.[4]

To the east of the house is the formal garden, a full acre of geometrically arranged plantings laid out by William Frost, an English landscape designer.[5] Both Mrs. Jackson and General Jackson are buried beneath the tomb in the southeast corner of the garden. Other members of the family and household are buried in the family plot nearby.

3. Ladies Hermitage Association, *The Hermitage: Home of Andrew Jackson*, p. 49.

4. Federal Writers' Project, *Tennessee: A Guide to the State*, p. 449.

5. Ladies Hermitage Association, *The Hermitage: Home of Andrew Jackson*, p. 22.

BIBLIOGRAPHY

Federal Writers' Project. *Tennessee: A Guide to the State*. New York: Viking Press, 1939.

Horn, Stanley F. "The Hermitage, Home of Andrew Jackson." In *Landmarks of Tennessee History*, edited by William T. Alderson and Robert M. McBride, pp. 5–21. Nashville: Tennessee Historical Society, Tennessee Historical Commission, 1965.

Horn, Stanley F. *The Hermitage: Home of Old Hickory*. Nashville: Ladies Hermitage Association, 1950.

Horn, Stanley F. "The Hermitage, Home of Andrew Jackson." *Antiques*, C, No. 3 (September 1971), 413–417.

Ladies Hermitage Association. *The Hermitage: Home of Andrew Jackson, A History and Guide*. Nashville: Ladies Hermitage Association, 1967.

Smith, J. Frazier. *White Pillars*. New York: Bramhall House, 1941.

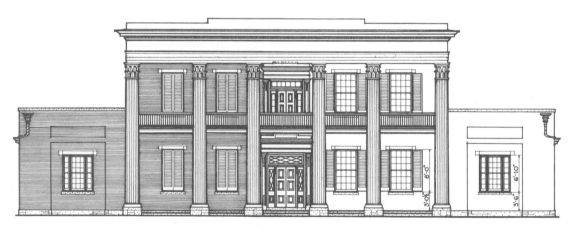

Front Elevation
HABS drawings by George D. Nevins

Magnolias shade the classic lines of the Jacksons' tomb in the southeast corner of the Hermitage garden.

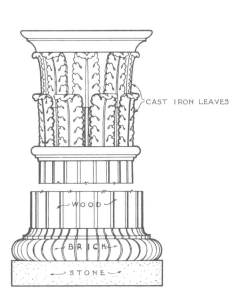

CAST IRON LEAVES

WOOD

BRICK

STONE

Detail of Column

The Hermitage
Nashville

Right Side Elevation, East
HABS drawing by Ralph Rosa

French wallpaper in the hall creates a sophisticated interior world in contrast to the workaday one outside.

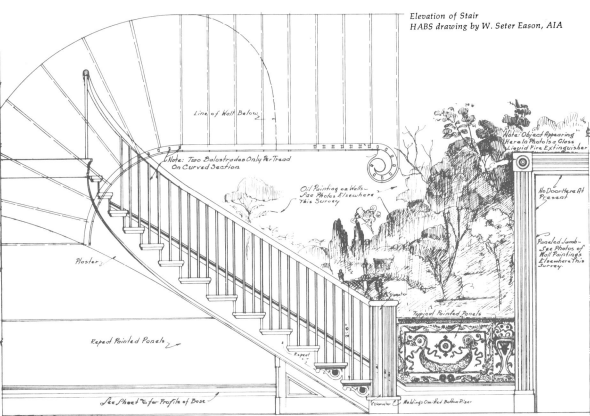

Elevation of Stair
HABS drawing by W. Seter Eason, AIA

The Hermitage
Nashville

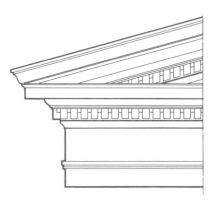

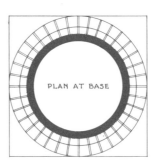

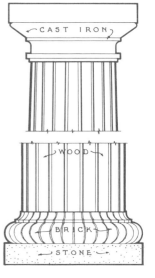

PLAN AT CAP

PLAN AT BASE

CAST IRON

WOOD

BRICK

STONE

*Details of Columns
and Pediment*

Rear Elevation

Jackson's common touch allowed the mantel of rough-cut hickory to grace his formal dining room.

Wessyngton

WESSYNGTON is in Robertson County, Tennessee, some five miles southeast of Springfield. Built in 1819 by Joseph Washington, the house has been owned continuously by the Washington family ever since. Mr. and Mrs. John T. Talbert are the present occupants.

Built in a simple Federal style, Wessyngton contains much of its original furniture, family portraits, and library. The garden designed by its first mistress, Mary Cheatham Washington, remains much as it was planned.

At the death of Joseph Washington in 1848, Wessyngton was inherited by his son, George Augustine Washington, who at his death in 1892 left it to his son Joseph Edwin Washington. Joseph Edwin Washington died in 1915 and with the death of his widow, Mary Bolling Kerns Washington, in 1938, the estate went to her children, George E. Washington, Anne W. Blagden, and Elizabeth Hotchkiss. In 1956 they formed the Wessyngton Company.

Wessyngton's original brick structure of 1819 consisted of a central hall flanked by a room on either side and a one-room ell projecting to the south from the east room. The same plan was repeated on the second floor. Soon after the original structure was built, a west wing, consisting of a passage and two rooms, was added. The unit formed an **L** so that the entire house was roughly in the shape of a **U**. A two-story back porch ran across the south and east sides of the rear of the house.

About the turn of the century, the pediments over the north and east porches were removed and roof lines were changed to the mansard form. A service wing was added to the southeast. A frame addition on the south of the house was added in 1905 as a temporary accommodation for the wedding guests at the marriage of Anne Washington to A. S. Blagden. The house was once painted white but is now faded back to the brick.

Wessyngton's first owner, Joseph, was descended from John Washington of Surry County, Virginia, who was the son of Sir John

Washington of Thrapston, Northampton County, England. Joseph Washington came to Tennessee from Virginia in 1796 and purchased land along Sulphur Fork. By his marriage to Mary Cheatham, he acquired another large tract adjoining his own. His estate became famous for the quality and quantity of its tobacco. His son, George Augustine Washington, was said to have been second only to the Khedive of Egypt in growing the largest amount of dark tobacco in the world.

BIBLIOGRAPHY

Brandau, Roberta Seawall, editor. *History of Homes and Gardens in Tennessee.* Nashville: Parthenon Press, 1936.

Cochran, Gifford A. *Grandeur in Tennessee.* New York: J. J. Augustin, 1946.

Nashville, Tennessee. Tennessee State Library and Archives. Washington Papers.

Tennessee. Robertson County. Office of County Court Clerk.

Tennessee. Robertson County. Office of the Register of Deeds.

A Federal eagle nestles on the corner of the main structure.

Wessyngton
Robertson County

The sprawl of two centuries records the history of a family.

Even the water tower has been given decorative treatment.

Castalian Springs
(Wynnewood)

CASTALIAN SPRINGS, 8½ miles east of Gallatin in Sumner County, is the largest surviving log structure of its period known in Tennessee. It was built as a tavern in 1828 and since 1834 has been used as a residence by the Wynne family, whose early prominence in the area drew many well-known historical figures to the house as guests.

In the early 1800s, Col. Alfred R. Wynne was a member of a stock company formed to build a tavern on the old stagecoach road leading from Baltimore to the Indian Nation in Middle Tennessee. The site chosen was on land belonging to Isaac Bledsoe and was known as the Bledsoe Spring salt lick—or Bledsoe's Lick— because the salt in the water had long made the spot a favorite grazing ground and watering place for buffalo, deer, and other wild animals. The builders selected it because of a nearby rivulet of pure sulphur water, thought by many to have health-giving properties. The builder of nearby Cragfont, Gen. James Winchester, whose daughter Almira married Col. Wynne, is said to have called the place Castalian Springs, in reference to Castalia, a fountain on Mount Parnassus sacred to the Muses.[1] In the small community that grew up at Bledsoe's Lick, so much mail came addressed to "Castalian Springs" that the name of the village was changed to Castalian Springs. The house which bears that name is also called Wynnewood. George Winchester Wynne, grandson of the builder, and Mrs. Wynne owned the property until December 1971, when they sold the house and fourteen acres to the State of Tennessee. Castalian Springs will be maintained, along with Cragfont and Rock Castle, as the third major state-owned historic site in Sumner County. Under an agreement with the Tennessee Historical Commission, the Bledsoe's Lick Historical Association will manage the property and develop it as a museum and visitors' center. The house and grounds were designated a national historic landmark in May 1972.

1. Ward Allen, "Cragfont: Grandeur on the Tennessee Frontier," p. 107.

Mr. and Mrs. Wynne continued as residents in a part of Castalian Springs until their recent deaths—Mrs. Wynne in 1972, Mr. Wynne in August 1973, at the age of 86.

As a tavern, Castalian Springs was not a success. In 1834, Col. Alfred R. Wynne bought out the other stockholders and converted the building into a residence.

There was no architect for the building: the hand-hewn logs were simply laid in the fashion customary at the time. The house today preserves its original plan and construction except for a few alterations. Originally, the structure was a two-storied log house with separate buildings for dining room and kitchen. It did not originally have a front porch, but steps led directly to the open "dog-trot," or breezeway. The Tennessee limestone

Rugged strength lay in the primary building material of the frontier.

Castalian Springs (Wynnewood)
Gallatin

The expansive old building represents earth-hugging security in the sweep of landscape.

foundations are 30 inches thick. The first-floor joists were hand-hewn on three sides, with the bark left on the underside. The walls are built of white oak logs except for those in the kitchen, which are black walnut. Floors are of random-sized poplar ash.

Between 1899 and 1910, when the building was maintained as a summer resort—with the sulphur water as a drawing card—a few structural changes were made. The roof of the back porch was lowered in 1898 and the porch was extended for the entire length of the house. The space between the old outside dining room and the main house was framed in to create a room more accessible to the kitchen. The front porch, added in 1894, was lengthened in 1898. A window was cut in the end of the extreme east room, about 1910. In some of the rooms, the exposed-beam ceilings have been covered and provisions for modern bathrooms have been made by enclosing areas within rooms. The original log walls have not been disturbed by the changes.

Col. Alfred Wynne was a friend of Andrew Jackson and shared Jackson's love of horse racing. Like many horse fanciers of the time, Wynne had his own racetrack at Castalian Springs. When Jackson died, Wynne planted a hickory tree in the yard at Castalian Springs in memory of his friend. In addition to Jackson, there were many other distinguished guests at Castalian Springs, among them Sam Houston. A less distinguished but well-known visitor spent the night there in 1882: under the name of Tom Howard, the notorious bank robber Jesse James enjoyed the Wynne hospitality while there to buy horses.

Allen, Ward. "Cragfont: Grandeur on the Tennessee Frontier." *Tennessee Historical Quarterly*, XXIII (June 1964), 103–120.
Brandau, Roberta Seawall. *History of Homes and Gardens of Tennessee.* Nashville: Parthenon Press, 1936.
Cisco, Jay Guy. *Historic Sumner County, Tennessee.* Nashville: Folk-Keelin Printing Company, 1909.
Cochran, Gifford A. *Grandeur in Tennessee.* New York: J. J. Augustin, 1946.
Durham, Walter T. *The Great Leap Westward: A History of Sumner County, Tennessee, From Its Beginnings to 1805.* Nashville: Parthenon Press, 1969.
Tennessee. Sumner County. Office of the Register.
Wynne, George Winchester. Interview. July 7, 1971.

The Carter House

THE Carter House at 1140 Columbia Avenue in Franklin, Williamson County, faces east on a level site betwen Strahl and Fowlkes streets. Now a museum owned by the State of Tennessee and cared for by the Carter House Association, the house figured prominently in the Civil War Battle of Franklin on November 30, 1864.

Built for Fountain Branch Carter in 1830, the building is a noteworthy example of the smaller, finely detailed houses built in Tennessee in the second quarter of the nineteenth century.

Nothing is known of the architect or builders, but the unsophisticated character of the structure would seem to indicate the work of local carpenters.

The Carter House was the residence on a farm of 288 acres. It has been restored to as near its original plan and construction as research can determine.

The L-shaped building is one-and-a-half stories tall, of natural brick, with an attached west wing of wood framing. The foundation is Tennessee limestone and the walls are solid brick with Flemish bond on the east front, English bond on the other exterior walls. Floor joists are hand-hewn, 10 to 12 inches deep, 2 ¼ to 5 ½ inches wide, at approximately 21 inches on center. The stepped parapets on the north and south walls have stone corbeling and are capped with stone. According to Dr. Moscow Carter, grandson of the man for whom it was built, these stepped parapets were torn down to the roof level during remodeling at some time after 1864, and the stone capping was used to border the front walk. The roof has a simple pitch and is now covered with modern asbestos shingles.

Careful restoration of the Carter House has reinstated the stepped parapets and their stone capping and stripped the house of dormer windows added during other remodelings, as were a frame wing on the south side and a porch on the north. An outside brick kitchen, the frame farm office, and a large brick smokehouse that were part of the original plan survive, but the barn and corn crib which were originally some fifty feet to the rear, and a cotton gin across the road to the south of the house, are no longer standing.

Brick chimneys stand at each end of the main wing and at the west end of the frame section of the building. The two main entry doors, each 2 by 7 feet 10 inches, have four panels each, with sidelights and fanlight above. Flooring is random-width ash and yellow poplar. There is a full basement under the masonry section of the house, approached by stairs on the porch.

The original owner, Fountain Branch Carter, had the house built on nineteen acres of land bought from Mr. and Mrs. Angus McPhail; Mrs. McPhail had inherited the tract from her father, Capt. Anthony Sharp, who received it as part of a grant from the State of North Carolina for his Revolutionary War services. Carter and his family were living in the house in 1864, when it became a strategic point in the Battle of Franklin.

On November 29, Union Gen. John M. Schofield slipped his troops past Confederate Gen. John B. Hood at Spring Hill. Schofield's plan was to reach Nashville, but on approaching Franklin, he found the bridges over the Harpeth River destroyed. Because of the delay that this caused and because of the proximity of his Confederate pursuers, he had to prepare at Franklin for attack. He left the defense of the southern edge of the town to Gen. Jacob D. Cox. Coming upon the Carter house at daybreak on November 30, General Cox awoke the family—Fountain Branch Carter, his eldest son, Moscow Branch Carter—a colonel in the Confederate army who was at the time at home on parole—four daughters, a daughter-in-law, and several grandchildren and servants—and told them that he would be using their house as temporary headquarters. The building faced the Columbia turnpike and stood on a hill which sloped away to Franklin on the north and to a level stretch on the south to Winstead Hill, where the Confederate Army prepared for attack. Neither General Cox nor the Carters thought that General Hood would charge the Union entrenchments in the Carter yard across a wide-open field. He did, however, and furious

Carter House
Franklin

fighting ensued. At the height of it, another Carter son, Capt. Theodoric (Tod) Carter, a staff officer of Confederate Gen. Thomas B. Smith, was mortally wounded. His elder brother Moscow was permitted to bring him off the field to die in the home he had left for military duty some two years earlier.

Fountain B. Carter lived in the house until 1871, when, at his death, it became the property of Moscow B. Carter. In 1896, Moscow Carter deeded the property to S. G. Mullins, who, after a few days, deeded it to O. E. Daniels, who held it until 1910, when it was acquired by Miss Robbie Hunter. At her death in 1946, the house passed to her brother, Bennett Hunter, who sold it to the State of Tennessee in 1951.

BIBLIOGRAPHY

Brandau, Roberta Seawall. *History of Homes and Gardens of Tennessee.* Nashville: Parthenon Press, 1936.

Davis, Louise. "House on a Haunted Hillside." The Nashville *Tennessean Magazine,* September 18, 1949, pp. 30–32.

Horn, Stanley F. *Tennessee's War, 1861–65.* Nashville: Tennessee Civil War Centennial Commission, 1965.

Huddleston, Ed. *The Civil War in Middle Tennessee.* Nashville: Parthenon Press, 1965.

South Elevation
HABS drawing by Barry S. Williams, 1971

A local builder's expedient is seen in the stepped-gable ends of the Carter House.

Carter House
Franklin

The severity of farm life as seen in functional outbuildings is relieved by an urbane interior.

Fairvue

FAIRVUE, four miles west of Gallatin on U.S. Highway 31-E in Sumner County, is a fine example of the classic-revival house built by wealthy Middle Tennesseans between 1830 and 1845. It is typical of the period which combined classic details in ornamentation with Georgian basic design to create homes of unusual grace and style.

Isaac Franklin, a wealthy cotton broker and slave trader, built Fairvue in 1832. An L-shaped wing to the south was added in 1839, and the place was described, some years later, as "what was proven by sworn testimony to have been, at that time, the finest country residence in Tennessee."[1] The mansion cost approximately $10,000 and its furnishings a similar amount. The several mantelpieces of black Kilkenny marble originally used in the double parlors and the dining room cost—it was said—$500 apiece.

In 1839, when he was fifty, Franklin married twenty-year-old Adelicia Hayes, daughter of Oliver B. Hayes, lawyer and leading citizen of Nashville. An honor graduate of Nashville Female Academy, Adelicia Hayes was considered "eminently qualified by birth, education and association to preside as mistress of such an establishment as . . . [Fairvue]."[2] Franklin died seven years later, leaving Adelicia enormously wealthy. In 1849, three years after her husband's death, Adelicia Hayes Franklin married Col. Joseph A. S. Acklen and soon began building Belmont Mansion—now Belmont College—in Nashville. Adelicia retained control of the Fairvue estate and other buildings throughout that marriage—which ended with Acklen's death in 1863—and in her subsequent marriage in 1867 to Dr. William Cheatham, with whom she executed a "marriage contract" assuring her the continuing right of ownership to all her properties.

In 1882, she sold Fairvue to Charles Reed of New York, a man well known in eastern

banking and racing circles. Reed kept Fairvue until 1908, converting the estate into a nursery for race horses. Between 1908 and its purchase in 1934 by William H. Wemyss, cofounder of General Shoe Corporation—now Genesco—Fairvue changed hands several times. Both house and furnishings reflected long-standing neglect and disrepair. Only four of the original mantels of Irish marble remained. Working with local carpenters, Mr. and Mrs. Wemyss restored Fairvue to its original form, and today it is carefully maintained.

No architect has been identified with Fairvue, but several workmen have. An inventory of the estate in 1847 identifies, among the slaves, skilled laborers in four trades: bricklayer, brick mason, carpenter, and blacksmith. There are references to the construction's being done largely by Franklin's own workers, supervised by capable craftsmen whom he hired.

The house is built of brick, and—somewhat unusual for Middle Tennessee houses of this period—it rests on brick foundations, rather than stone. It stands two-and-a-half stories tall, a U-shaped main block measuring 45 feet by 64 feet with an L-addition of 32 feet by 74 feet. The east and west faces of the main wing are Flemish bond, with common bond used elsewhere. Four Ionic columns and two pilasters appear on the first and second levels of porches on the east and west. Two large brick chimneys rise on the north and south faces of the main wing, with another chimney on the old kitchen wall. Areaways open into a basement. The gabled roof is copper sheeting with standing seams. The entry hall, with openings and porches on the east and west sides, contains a central stairway flanked by two rooms on either side on both the first and second floors. Off the first-floor hall are a double parlor, dining room, secondary hall, and living room. The second level of the main wing contains four bedrooms divided by two bathrooms. The upstairs hall contains a service stair. The attached wing on the second end, forming the U-shape, contains the kitchen, breakfast room, and a small winding stair, with

1. Douglas Anderson, *The Historic Blue Grass Line*, pp. 78–82.
2. *Ibid.*

An almost Venetian elegance looks out across a Middle Tennessee landscape.

Fairvue
Gallatin

The grandeur of the long main hall still greets visitors to Fairvue.

An icehouse and slave quarters are forlorn survivors of an earlier age.

bedrooms and study above. Ash flooring is used downstairs, with poplar upstairs.

A tall brick fence originally enclosed various outbuildings and front and rear lawns and gardens. The original outbuildings—all of brick —included a kitchen, smokehouse, barn, carriage house and stables, hostler's house, blacksmith and carpenter shops, a mill, overseer's house, and a dozen or so slave houses. In the large kitchen garden were a small playhouse for children and a conservatory for winter-sensitive plants. A circular brick icehouse with a conical roof stood in the flower garden.

Between 1882 and 1908, when Charles Reed maintained the place as a horse farm, great sections of the brick fence enclosing lawns and gardens were taken up, the brick being used to build several two-story horse barns. A portion of the fence has been restored and stands today on its original foundation, enclosing a well-kept garden and the original circular icehouse.

BIBLIOGRAPHY

Anderson, Douglas. *The Historic Blue Grass Line.* Nashville: Nashville-Gallatin Interurban Railway: 1913.

Brandau, Roberta Seawell. *History of Homes and Gardens in Tennessee.* Nashville: Parthenon Press, 1936.

Stephenson, Wendell Holmes. *Isaac Franklin, Slave Trader and Planter of the Old South.* Gloucester, Massachusetts: Peter Smith, 1968.

Succession of Isaac Franklin. Prepared by Mrs. Joseph A. S. Acklen's counsel for use of Supreme Court. N.p., 1851.

Tennessee. Sumner County. Register of Deeds.

Rattle and Snap

(The Polk-Granbery House)

RATTLE and Snap, on a hilltop 7½ miles west of Columbia on State Highway 43 in Maury County, is a fine example of the lavish scale on which many Southern houses were built between 1845 and 1860. Often referred to as "the most monumental house in Tennessee," the house is particularly noteworthy for its ornamental iron work and for the fine detail of its Corinthian columns, both inside and out.

Although none of the original outbuildings remain and the present landscaping makes no attempt to follow the elaborate plan of the original, the house itself has stood virtually unchanged since its erection in 1845.

Rattle and Snap was built for George Polk, youngest of the nine sons of William Polk, a North Carolinian who was appointed surveyor-general of the Middle District of Tennessee in 1784 and, through speculation in land, became one of the largest landholders in Tennessee. The tract on which the house stands amounted originally to 5,648 acres, and William Polk named the property Rattle and Snap because he had won it from the governor of North Carolina in a gambling game of that name, said to have been played with beans. Four of Polk's sons built substantial homes on the tract: Lucius built Hamilton Place; Rufus King, Westwood; Leonidas built Ashwood, which his brother Andrew later bought and enlarged; and George built Rattle and Snap. Where their properties joined, the brothers built St. John's Episcopal Church, where all but Leonidas are buried.

The architect for Rattle and Snap is not known. A letter written by George Polk's daughter, Caroline Polk Horten, states that the house was built by slaves skilled in the building trades.[1] The materials used were brick and stone, the brick made on the place and the stone for the portico brought by wagon from Cincinnati. The house itself appears to be built of native stone.

Rattle and Snap is L-shaped, two-and-a-half stories tall, the main wing measuring 66 feet by 54 feet, the ell, 54 feet by 20 feet. Four porches face north, east, west, and south. On the north porch are ten Corinthian columns with projecting bay; on the east, a small entryway with four columns; west, a cast-iron balcony; on the south is a frame two-story porch with gallery along both wings of the ell. Six brick chimneys served fireplaces inside. Cornices are classical Corinthian.

Special decorative features of the interior are ornamental plaster work on ceilings and cornices and Corinthian columns dividing the parlor, entrance hall, and cross hall. Interior flooring is wide-board poplar.

The Polks lived at Rattle and Snap until 1867, when the house was deeded to J. J. Granbery. The Granbery family sold it in 1919 to W. P. Ridley and W. A. Dale. During their ownership, the house was unoccupied except for a caretaker. In 1950, Ridley's heir, Mrs. Charles W. Jewell, bought the interests of Dale's heir. In 1953, Mr. and Mrs. Jewell deeded the house and 113.315 acres to Mr. and Mrs. Oliver M. Babcock. Under the personal supervision of Babcock and his carpenter, Spence Parsons, modern heating, lighting, and plumbing were installed, with a minimum amount of change to the original structure.

The name *Granbery* in connection with Rattle and Snap is found spelled in several different ways, but local histories used this spelling most frequently.

1. Caroline Polk Horten to Mrs. T. P. Yeatman, Yeatman-Polk Papers, Manuscripts Division, Tennessee State Library and Archives, Nashville, Tennessee.

Rattle and Snap
Columbia

The varied possibilities suggested by some builder's guide to refined taste have been demonstrated in profusion.

BIBLIOGRAPHY

Brandau, Roberta Seawell, editor. *History of Homes and Gardens of Tennessee*. Nashville: Parthenon Press, 1936.

Cochran, Gifford A. *Grandeur in Tennessee*. New York: J. J. Augustin, 1946.

Fort, Chloe Frierson. "A New Life for Rattle and Snap." The Nashville *Tennessean Magazine*, April 25, 1954, pp. 24–28.

Garrett, Jill K. "St. John's Church, Ashwood." *Tennessee Historical Quarterly*, XXIX (Spring 1970), 3–23.

Nashville, Tennessee. Manuscripts Division. Tennessee State Library and Archives. Yeatman-Polk Papers.

Raleigh, North Carolina. Wake County Records, vol. 23, p. 46. Will of William Polk, probated February 1834.

Smith, J. Frazer. *White Pillars*. New York: William Helburn, Inc., 1941.

The Adolphus Heiman House

THE house of the architect Adolphus Heiman at 900 Jefferson Street, Nashville, was built from about 1845 to 1850. It is currently occupied by the Tennessee Baptist Missionary and Educational Convention Headquarters.

Although Heiman was the outstanding architect working in the Middle Tennessee area after the death of William Strickland, he built himself a rather small "villa" in the Italian style. It is, of course, an excellent demonstration of the sort of house which he would have built for middle-class clients at the time. It is very close to the type of house which A. J. Downing designated in his pattern books as a Gate Lodge in the Italian style. Such "lodges," Downing tells us, "should be supported, and partially concealed, by trees and foliage . . . and should be considered part of a whole, grouping with other objects in rural landscape."[1] Nothing whatever of Heiman's landscaping survives, although the building still dominates the pleasant hill on which it was set.

Today we see the structure drastically changed, scarcely more than a shell, and with the tall windows of its Tuscan tower boarded up, giving it an unpleasant blind effect. Such towers always called for a sloping roof, rather than a flat one. The decorative cast-iron work which may once have graced the original side porch as it now does the front is represented by only a fragment in place. A handsome front door frame survives, but the side entrance has been marred by the addition of a highly inappropriate Federal style door and frame of recent date. The front door itself, along with decorative entablatures over the larger windows, seems to date from the 1870s. The side porch of concrete is a fairly recent addition. Interiors have largely been rearranged.

BIBLIOGRAPHY

Frank, John G. "Adolphus Heiman: Architect and Soldier." *Tennessee Historical Quarterly*, V (March 1946), 35–57.

Parrent, H. Clinton, Jr. "Adolphus Heiman and the Building Methods of Two Centuries." *Tennessee Historical Quarterly*, XII (September 1953), 204–212.

1. Andrew J. Downing, *A Treatise on the Theory and Practice of Landscape Gardening, Adapted to North America*, pp. 360–361.

Closely spaced brackets under the eaves are one of the few reminders of Adolphus Heiman's taste.

Belmont

(Col. J. A. S. Acklen House; Belmont College, Acklen Hall)

IN 1850, when Col. and Mrs. J. A. S. Acklen built Belmont, it was considered one of the finest private residences in the South. Belmont was constructed in the manner of an Italian Renaissance villa, with Greek-revival detail, and is thought to have been designed by William Strickland.

Its moving force, and the one person integral to its history, was Adelicia Acklen, a woman of extraordinary character, even by today's standards.

Belmont faces south at what is now Belcourt and 17th Avenue, South, in Nashville, on a plot of land bought by Adelicia in 1849, shortly before her marriage to Colonel Acklen, who was her second husband.

Born Adelicia Hayes in 1819, she was married at twenty to Isaac Franklin, a millionaire cotton broker and slave trader thirty years her senior, and went to live at Fairvue, Franklin's Sumner County estate. Adelicia's social distinction, culture, and charm helped to make Fairvue a showplace of the Nashville area. When Franklin died, in 1846, Adelicia was said to be the wealthiest woman in the United States, owning Fairvue (which she kept until 1882), seven plantations in Louisiana, and 50,000 acres of land in Texas.

On May 8, 1849, she married Joseph Alexander Smith Acklen, a dashing young lawyer from Huntsville, Alabama. At the beginning of the Civil War, Acklen was interested in making every possible contribution to the Confederacy. On a trip to his plantations in Louisiana in 1863, he died of a fever.

Four years later, in an outdoor wedding at Belmont that attracted wide attention, Adelicia Hayes Franklin Acklen married Dr. William Cheatham. What was perhaps the most distinctive feature of the ceremony was not widely known, but it illustrated Adelicia's strong sense of independence: it was a "Marriage Contract" executed by the bride and groom, assuring Adelicia the continuing right of ownership to all her properties, including Belmont.

In 1887, when she was 68, Adelicia Cheatham sold Belmont to Lewis T. Baxter, who, in turn, sold it to Miss Ida E. Hood and Miss Susan L. Heron, both of Philadelphia. Two years later, Adelicia died, having lived a life filled with drama and romance. She is still a legend in the Nashville area, and she may be the only Nashvillian to have been presented to Queen Victoria.

After Adelicia's death, Belmont ceased to be an elegant residence and became a series of educational institutions. Miss Hood and Miss Heron became the founders, joint owners, and principals of Belmont Junior College, which they established there after 1890. In 1911, on their retirement, Ward Seminary moved to the Belmont campus, and the institution became known as Ward-Belmont School, a junior college for women. In February 1951, the property was sold to the Tennessee Baptist Convention, and Ward-Belmont became Belmont College, a coeducational, four-year college under the supervision of the Tennessee Baptist Convention.

After Belmont was built by the Acklens, the original estate was enlarged through subsequent purchases and became known for extensive parks and gardens. No plans or drawings of any kind have been found for the original two-story building, with its square central portion flanked by symmetrical wings on either side. The walls are of stone and brick, the trim and roof, of wood. The wings were heavily adorned with cast iron. Ornamental cast iron was used extensively as a special decorative feature at Belmont, as were Venetian-glass transoms and sidelights and door glass. There are two porches with balconies above, supported by columns 13 inches in diameter. The main recessed porch has a granite floor and the columns supporting its balcony are 27 inches in diameter. An octagonal cupola centers on the main hall. Heavy cornices with dentils and modillions appear throughout.

The house faced south, toward gently sloping gardens, and the present grounds follow some of the lines of the original landscape pattern. The five original cast-iron summer houses remain. The distinctive water tower was used as a

Belmont
Nashville

signal tower by Federal forces during the Civil War. From 1929 to 1952, it housed the War Memorial of World War I, a gift of carillon bells from the alumnae of Belmont College, Ward Seminary, and Ward-Belmont. Statues collected by the Acklens in Europe were placed throughout the gardens. They included biblical characters and heroic figures of the gods and goddesses of classical mythology.[1]

Although William Strickland is traditionally regarded as the architect of Belmont, nothing has been found to authenticate this tradition. However, the building's proportion and massing are in many ways related to Strickland's known work on the Tennessee State Capitol and St. Mary's Cathedral. Belmont has the same

1. Ivar Lou Myhr Duncan, "A History of Belmont," p. 10.

compelling simplicity of form, and there is little that is awkard or unresolved in its design. The general proportions of the Corinthian distyle-in-antis portico at Belmont invite comparison with the similar treatment of the Ionic portico at St. Mary's. The sophistication with which Greek profile and moldings are handled recalls the manner of detail in the State Capitol. The Corinthian columns and rich cornice with acanthus leaves and eagles on the interior, while Italianate, seem to conform to the basic proportional formula in Strickland's known work. The manner in which the Great Hall at Belmont is handled recalls the Banking Room of Strickland's Second Bank of the United States (1819–1824). And such masterful work as the ingenious stairway, superbly integrated into the complex interior composition, suggests that Strickland did indeed participate in the design.

A few relics survive from the maze of statues, hedges, and gazebos that once spread across the landscape.

Belmont
Nashville

BIBLIOGRAPHY

Brandau, Roberta Seawell, editor. *History of Homes and Gardens of Tennessee.* Nashville: Parthenon Press, 1936.

Cochran, Gifford A. "Belmont." In *Grandeur in Tennessee,* by Gifford A. Cochran, pp. 117–121. New York: J. J. Augustin, 1946.

Duncan, Ivar Lou Myhr. "A History of Belmont College." Pámphlet, n.d.

Federal Writers' Project. *Tennessee. A Guide to the State.* New York: Viking Press, 1939.

Gilchrist, Agnes A. *William Strickland. Architect and Engineer, 1788–1854.* Philadelphia: University of Philadelphia Press, 1950.

Smith, J. Frazer. *White Pillars.* New York: William Helburn, 1941.

Tennessee. Davidson County. Register's Office.

Legend has it that Adelicia designed the stair for her own dramatic—and unaccompanied—descent in crinoline to parties in the atrium.

Worker's House

THE small worker's house in Nashville is an example of the Italian villa style reduced to basic essentials. It was built of brick, about 1850. Some twenty to thirty similar houses of wood or brick survive in Nashville side streets off Jefferson, near the Adolphus Heiman House. The building shown here is typical of its kind— the modest small structure so difficult to preserve, the first to disappear with the onrush of time.

The entrance vestibule shown in this example is a bit unusual, and there is a well-proportioned rounded door frame with a modest fanlight. Relatively heavy eaves with doubled brackets are the only other ostentation.

Such tiny houses, of two, three, or four rooms, were often extended with wooden, tin-roofed "summer kitchens" and various lean-tos.

The bow-and-arrow motif of a wrought-iron fence, put up to protect the yard from stray livestock, repeats the shape of the rounded door frame.

Two Rivers

(David H. McGavock House)

TWO RIVERS Mansion is the second and principal house erected on Two Rivers Farm, so named because of its position at the junction of the Stone's and Cumberland rivers. The house faces east, 220 yards west of McGavock Pike on McGavock Lane in Donelson, Davidson County.

Built in 1859 by David H. McGavock on land inherited by his wife, Willie E., from her father, William Harding, the mansion is one of the earliest, most significant, and best-preserved of the early Italianate houses in Middle Tennessee. A small, white-painted brick house southeast of the mansion was built in 1802 by William Harding and was the original residence at Two Rivers Farm.

Until its sale to the Metropolitan Government of Nashville and Davidson County in 1966, Two Rivers was owned by the McGavock family. The last to live there was Mary Louise Bransford McGavock, who received the property as a wedding present when she married Spence McGavock in 1928. In 1933, the couple moved from Two Rivers to Melrose to be with Mrs. McGavock's widowed father. After the death of her husband in 1936 and that of her father in 1938, Mary Louise McGavock continued to live at Melrose until 1955, when she moved back to Two Rivers, which had remained vacant in the interim.

No plans or drawings of any kind are known to have existed at the time the house was built or to survive to the present day.

The identity of the architect has not been established. Two published sources—May Winston Caldwell's *Historical and Beautiful Country Homes near Nashville, Tennessee,* and *History of Homes and Gardens of Tennessee,* edited by Roberta S. Brandau—provide conflicting identities of the possible architect. The Caldwell account—whose pages are unnumbered—says that "Mr. McGavock was his own architect and builder, cutting with his own mill all the timber from trees on the place." The later Brandau book observes (p. 180) that "the main mansion house . . . is said to have been planned by the architect, William Strickland, in 1859."

It should be observed, however, that William Strickland died on April 7, 1854, and had been buried in the walls of the Tennessee State Capitol for five years when Two Rivers was erected in 1859. It is conceivable that the author may have had Strickland's son, Francis, in mind, but the latter's name has not been encountered in any reference to Two Rivers. In the absence of any documentation whatever at the present time, it is impossible to identify the architect of the mansion. The great sophistication apparent in the design, however, and the refinement and integration of its component details suggest the hand of someone other than an amateur. No evidence exists to suggest that David H. McGavock had the benefit of any prior or comparable experience in designing the house. At the same time, the details employed throughout the house and the manner of their composition are not those customarily seen in William Strickland's known work.

Published sources agree that the brick to build Two Rivers was made on the estate, the stone was quarried there by the McGavock slaves, and the timber was cut and prepared at the McGavock sawmill. A cornerstone reads: "John L. Stewart, Builder of Stone Work, 1859."[1]

Two Rivers is an L-shaped brick building two stories tall, measuring 106 feet by 66 feet, with full basement. The walls are of solid brick, with stone foundations.

The simple pitched roof is metal-covered with stand-up seams approximately 15 inches apart. There are six brick chimneys with stone caps. The wooden cornice has sculptured brackets on the frieze.

The two main entry doors are wooden and panelled, large and ornate. Other exterior doors are four-panelled, with transoms.

The two upper levels are connected by interior stairways, and stairs to the basement are on the south porch. The original kitchen was

1. Leona Taylor Aiken, *Donelson, Tennessee. Its History and Landmarks,* p. 237.

Two Rivers
Nashville

166   at the end of the west wing of the basement, serving the first level by dumbwaiter. The original random-width flooring still exists on the first level, with modern narrow oak flooring on the second. The basement floor is of brick, dirt, and wood.

Special decorative features of the interior are elaborate moldings at the door heads and jambs on the first floor, which also has 16-inch-high baseboards.

There are only sporadic references to alterations made to Two Rivers. When Mary Louise Bransford married Spence McGavock in 1928 and received from him Two Rivers as a wedding gift, her father had the house completely redecorated. Bathrooms were added, and electricity and steam were installed. A tornado struck in March 1933 and damaged the roofs and porches, sending debris crashing down to destroy one of the stairways.

Prior to her return to Two Rivers from Melrose in 1955, Mrs. McGavock had the mansion redecorated. An elevator was later added.

Mrs. McGavock died in 1965, bequeathing a principal portion of the Two Rivers estate to the Vanderbilt University School of Medicine and Vanderbilt University Hospital. Nashville's First American National Bank was named executor of the estate and authorized to sell the property. With a federal grant for fifty percent of the cost of acquiring the 447 acres, the Metropolitan Government of Nashville and Davidson County purchased the estate on October 20, 1966, for $995,000. Thirty acres has been alloted for a new high school, and forty-five acres will be develeoped into thoroughfares. The remainder of the area is being planned as a park. The mansion and the 1802 white-painted brick house are to be preserved as historic museums.

BIBLIOGRAPHY

Aiken, Leona Taylor. "Two Rivers." In *Donelson, Tennessee. Its History and Landmarks*, by Leona Taylor Aiken. Kingsport, Tenn.: n. p., 1968, pp. 231–241.

Brandau, Roberta Seawell, editor. "Two Rivers Farm, Nashville." In *History of Homes and Gardens of Tennessee*, edited by Roberta S. Brandau. Nashville: Parthenon Press, 1936.

Caldwell, May Winston. "Two Rivers." In *Historical and Beautiful Country Homes near Nashville, Tennessee*. Nashville: Brandon Printing Co., 1911.

Clayton, W. W. *History of Davidson County, Tennessee, with Illustrations and Biographical Sketches of Its Prominent Men*. Philadelphia: J. W. Lewis & Co., 1880.

Federal Writers' Project. Tennessee. *A Guide to the State*. New York: Viking Press, 1939.

Rudy, Jeanette C. *Historical Two Rivers*. Nashville: Blue and Gray Press, Inc., 1973.

Tennessee. Davidson County. County Clerk's Office.

Tennessee. Davidson County. Register's Office.

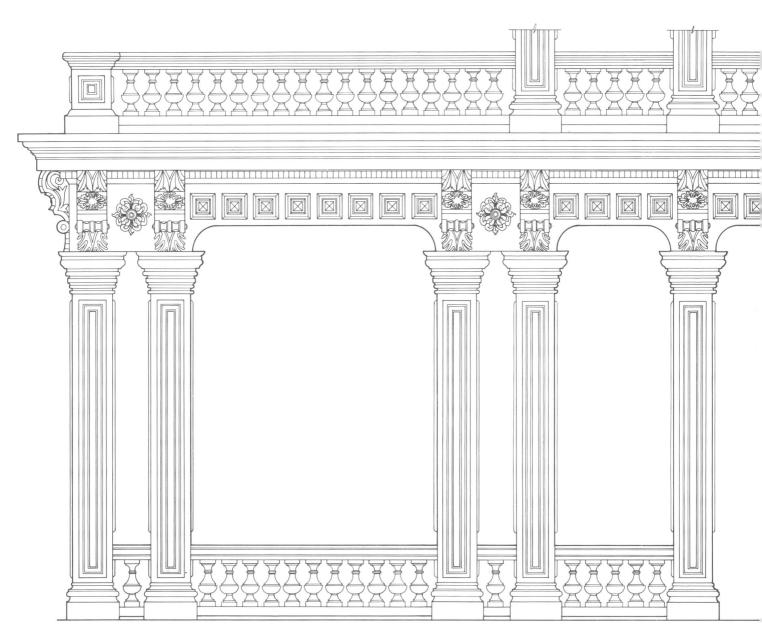

Partial North Porch Elevation
HABS drawing by William H. Edwards and Patrick W. Crawford, 1970

Two Rivers
Nashville

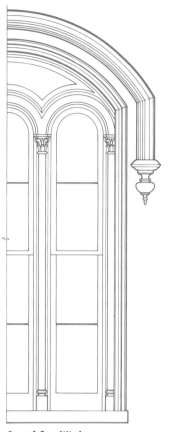

Second-floor Window
Exterior, North Elevation

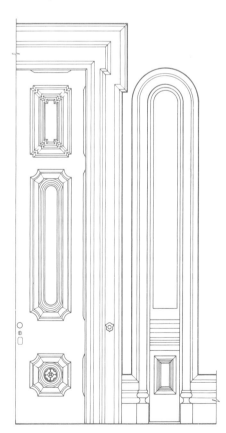

First-floor Door
Interior, North Elevation
HABS drawings by William H. Edwards, 1970

Epilogue

Even in a book twice the size of this one, it would have been impossible to include all of the superb photographs and architectural drawings made of Middle Tennessee buildings by the Historic American Buildings Survey team in 1970 and 1971.

Further information about Middle Tennessee survey records and illustrations—those included in this book as well as those for which there was no space—can be obtained by writing to the Historic American Buildings Survey, National Park Service, Department of the Interior, Washington, D.C., 20240.

The HABS archives in the Prints and Photographs Division of the U.S. Library of Congress contain more than 30,000 measured drawings, 40,000 photographs, and 10,000 pages of documentation for more than 16,000 historic buildings in the United States. Copies of these records may be ordered from the Photoduplication Service, Library of Congress, Washington, D.C., 20540. Copies of newer records not yet deposited in the Library of Congress are available from the National Park Service, Washington, D.C., 20240.

Buildings included in this book are identified by a survey number which appears below. The name of the structure and the survey number should be included in requests for further information or reproductions.

Survey Number	Structure
Tenn. 51	Tennessee State Capitol
Tenn. 33	Tennessee State Penitentiary
Tenn. 38	Federal Building (Clarksville)
Tenn. 35	Poston Buildings (Clarksville)
Tenn. 16	S. D. Morgan and Co. (Nashville)
Tenn. 39	Grange Warehouse (Clarksville)
Tenn. 20	Second Avenue, North (Nashville)
Tenn. 22	Werthan Bag Corporation (Nashville)
Tenn. 36	Bear Spring Furnace (Dover)
Tenn. 23	Ryman Auditorium (Nashville)
Tenn. 21	Union Station (Nashville)
Tenn. 24	Public Arcade (Nashville)
Tenn. 13	St. Mary's Cathedral, Roman Catholic (Nashville)
Tenn. 17	First (Downtown) Presbyterian Church (Nashville)
Tenn. 64	Zion Presbyterian Church (Columbia)
Tenn. 135	Holy Trinity Episcopal Church (Nashville)
Tenn. 18	University of Nashville—Children's Museum (Nashville)
Tenn. 19	Jubilee Hall, Fisk University (Nashville)
Tenn. 11	Vanderbilt University Gymnasium (Nashville)
Tenn. 34	West Side Row, Vanderbilt University (Nashville)
Tenn. 131	Rock Castle (Hendersonville)
Tenn. 65	Hays-Kiser House (Antioch)
Tenn. 14	Travellers' Rest (Nashville)
Tenn. 82	Cragfont (Gallatin)
Tenn. 31	Oaklands (Murfreesboro)
Tenn. 52	The Hermitage (Nashville)
Tenn. 32	Wessyngton (Robertson County)
Tenn. 81	Castalian Springs—Wynnewood (Gallatin)
Tenn. 37	Carter House (Franklin)
Tenn. 80	Fairvue (Gallatin)
Tenn. 63	Rattle and Snap (Columbia)
Tenn. 25	Adolphus Heiman House (Nashville)
Tenn. 56	Belmont (Nashville)
Tenn. 26	Worker's House (Nashville)
Tenn. 15	Two Rivers (Nashville)